Wounds

to Wisdom...

THE SURVIVOR SERIES
Volume 2

COMPILED BY TAMIKO LOWRY PUGH
Stories By: Tamara Charles – Venus Miller - Yamma Brown
Alexander - Detra Williams - Lakesia Muhammad - Roderick
Cunningham - Kimberly Claborn - April Kelley - Duntenia
Fitts - Lakeisha Christian - Pamela Morgan – Kanorris Davis

Published by Still Standing Publishing Company
Book Cover Design: Still Standing Publishing Design Team
Front Cover Photo Credit: Cornell McBride Photography

Printed in the United States of America

ISBN-13: 978-0999336229
ISBN-10: 0999336223

Dedication

This book is dedicated to domestic violence victims and survivors all over the world. There is purpose behind the pain. God will turn your wounds into wisdom and one day your will say... "Wow, I Survived!

No matter what it is you go through in life, remember that all things work together for the good for those who love God and who are called according to His purpose.
Romans 8:27-29

"The human race tends to remember the abuses to which it has been subjected rather than the endearments. What's left of kisses? Wounds, however, leave scars."
— Bertolt Brecht

Contents

WOUND

***

MERRIAM-WEBSTER DEFINES A WOUND AS

An injury in which the surface of something is torn, pierce, cut, or otherwise broken. Hurt.

Preface

By Tamiko Lowry Pugh

Though Wounded, I Was Not Destroyed... I Survived!

Think of a young child playing on a playground. As she runs, jumps and climbs she is so filled with the joy of interacting with the other children that the excitement of the moment brings laughter to her spirit and a smile on her face. So of course, she doesn't consider that she will get hurt.

Then suddenly, another child comes over and pushes her down (mistakenly or intentional). She falls to the ground badly scraping her knee which causes her so much pain that she begins to cry. Naturally, her mother runs to her aid to console her; cleaning the wound, carefully bandaging it. Then over time, nurturing the wound until it one day heals.

However, as she grew older, the scar remained as a reminder of that day on the playground. Though she tried everything that she could to try to make it fade nothing has ever made it disappear. So, she just frustratingly conceals it.

Many of us are like the little girl in the story, throughout the course of our lives we are often faced with many situations and circumstances that may cause us to become wounded—physically, emotionally, mentally, financially and even spiritually. These bumps and bruises we tend to carry with us along our journey; which seem to never go away.

*Identify://*Generally, when we speak of *wounds* we tend to gravitate toward thinking about only the physical wounds. However, we must consider that we are made up of more than just physical mass. Therefore, wounding may occur as matters of the heart (*emotional*), matters of the mind (*mental*), matters of the soul (*spiritual*) or matters of our livelihood (*financial*)—all of which can affect our overall wellness. By properly identifying with all areas of your life you will begin to discover the essential tools needed along your journey toward the peacefulness of true survivorship.

Source:// It's important that we take full responsibility for examining the anatomy of our wounds so that we will grasp ahold of and embrace the true power of our healing and wellness. Gaining an understanding of the source of our wounds also helps us to become more aware of *"clear-and-present-danger."* In other words, by recognizing repetitive source patterns, we become more mindful of our choices in the present.

Though our wounds may derive from many sources [intentional or unintentional] and in some cases, have a lingering painful effect, they serve as learning scars that teach us throughout our journey to wisdom.

HIDDEN RAGE
By Kanorris Davis

This poem was inspired by the surroundings of everyday life. Stories shared with me from friends, family and everyday strangers; being that person someone could easily talk to leaving the judgement absent of the mind. The tongue is a powerful thing. I've always heard so, I keep in mind to understand the burdens that wears on another's mind and heart. Loving the feeling that people could easily talk to me inspires me to create a feeling that is mutual through writing. It's the way that I communicate with others using a different voice; the voice that resides in your mind, our conscious!

Hidden Rage, The Poem

Drawn apart from her mind, crying for justice but true pain trials her heart, she leaves a house tending to the world she treats as home; constantly checking her phone praying and hoping that the anger and abuse leaves her alone, long gone the image of herself conscious has disappeared over the years, mentally abused and confused with the purpose of her true being, steady she remains with the rain even on her sunny days, trapped like an animal she wanders life as a maze dying for a quick escape, no grass so she couldn't compare it to the other side, wishing she never cut ties with those who warned her ahead of time, a painted smile that tarnished with the weather, even on the sunniest days she'd wear a sweater as if she were hiding her temple, body covered in black and blue with the assertion to others that she was loved, gone away from his home to long she returns only to vanish, he walks away from home leaving behind an abused soul; speaking, laughing, and loving all the strangers around, everybody that he has met says, "he's one of the nicest guys around.", as she dies everyday feeling as if she's loving a stranger; frustration and tears start to conquer her fears, so much rage in her eyes silents her conscious, she's gone mad, tired of the blows thrown at her as if she were a punching bag with no feelings, she loads a metal piece she purchased from a local pawn shop, lying to the dealer of the true cause to bring herself peace, loaded two bullets saying to herself, "one for you and one for me", patiently waiting for his arrival, she sits there in agony as if nothing was wrong, he enters the house shows her no attention, walks by her as if her existence mirrored a ghost, just a normal night he had thought; like the nights before they had fought, lying on the floor bleeding from head to toe she looks up wiping tears as he constantly yells, being towered by what the world thought was a gentle foe, the fragrance he wore she didn't adore, smelling like booze and cheap perfume, she reaches under the couch pillow as he turns to continue a life he loves, seeing a glimpse of her life she visioned nothing extraordinary, she couldn't remember the last night he made her smile, a lost child she was living in this world never finding her way until this night, unwanted courage killed two souls; she fired aiming for the head but she pierced his shoulder he then turns in rage charging towards her; she fires again last bullet she seen travel through his brain, she dropped to her knees shaking violently, the neighbors across the street runs over with urgency yet cautious to the situation, kicking in the door only to see two bodies one breathless and the other on all four, rushing to her seeing she had been tortured they held her with comfort as she cried, forever; for the rest of her days she never loved again, the night she'd never forget set her free, locked mentally terrified to the world she could never enjoy another man attempt of a hug as she'd flinch from the fear of being hit....

Chapter One

UNBROKEN, STILL I SMILE
By Tamara Charles

*I will turn all the negatives into something positive because
I am "Unbroken, Still I Smile.
~Tamara Charles*

As a 3 time, domestic violence survivor my goal is to
Empower and Uplift other women that may be going through
a domestic violence relationship and need that extra push
and guidance to turn their abusive relationship into
something positive. I had to acknowledge the fact that I was
facing these challenges and the affect that it had on my mind,
body, and soul. I had to take the first step on healing and
restoring myself by putting God first in my life. As you read
my story, you will gain the strength to take your first step.
You will not be ashamed of being judged. You will be free
and love yourself all over again. Once you rid yourself of the
negative lifestyle, all the good things that are meant for you
will be delivered to you and doors will start opening up. As
you read my story, you will find through all the obstacles,
you're Unbroken, Still you Smile. I look at myself in the
mirror all the time and continuously reassure myself. I Love
me and I Love you my sisters. We are in this fight together
and together we can make a difference. Let Go of all the hurt
and pain and Let God in.

Mr. Child Support Man: I met Mr. Child Support man
through some mutual friends in high school. When we met, I

had no attraction to him at all. I had my group of girlfriends who were dating his group of friends. That's how it all started. I was fifteen years old in my senior year when we met at the Officers Club. This was a popular under twenty-one club that everyone around my community would go to.

Mr. Child Support Man expressed his interest in me to one of my girlfriends at the time but, I told my friend that I was not interested in him because I was not attracted to him and he was not my type. Mr. Child Support man and his friends would come down from Cambridge, Massachusetts after school with his boys to come and hang out with my girlfriends in my hometown of Lynn, Massachusetts. As time went on and after being pressured to give him a chance. I did just that but, deep down in my heart, I knew I didn't want to be with him in a girlfriend/boyfriend type of relationship. Seeing

that my friends had their boyfriends, I decided to give in and give him a chance. I didn't know anything about being in a relationship, let alone having a boyfriend. We did go to each other's Junior and Senior prom in high school.

Mr. Child Support man was into me more than I was into him and it was obvious to everyone. This is where the abusiveness started. It all began with him being jealous and controlling. He wanted me to act a certain way because my friends were more of a girlfriend to his boys and I was acting like as if I were a single girl. I was fifteen-sixteen years old. What did I know about being in a relationship? I was still a child whom at the time thought when you French kissed a boy that you would get pregnant. I was that teenage girl who would front to my friends that I was already sexually active but knowing I wasn't. Mr. Child Support man's jealousy started getting so bad that he began to put his hands on me.

I remember the first time he physically abused me. I was sixteen years old, in my senior year of high school. We were hanging out with our group of friends and drinking alcohol that night. One of his friends had shown interest in me, and he knew that. So, when we got to his parents' house, he brought it up and started to verbally down talk me, accusing me of enjoying the attention his friend was giving me. It was that night that he slapped me for the first time across my face. I cried, and he said he was sorry and that he would never do it again. That never doing it again began to happen more often until it started to be a norm in our relationship. We would break up and get back together. But, deep down inside I knew I didn't love him. I was just afraid of hurting his feelings because I was scared of what he would do to me.

He was a guy that grew up in a household of both of his parents even though, his parents were still married they slept in separate rooms at times. He was living the street life and selling drugs. Even though I knew what he was doing was wrong, I was OK with it. I thought it was cool at age sixteen and seventeen to be with a drug dealer that was making sure your hair, nails were done and buying me clothes.

We went to the Best Western Hotel almost every weekend, and he would take me to the outlets to buy me nice clothes and jewelry. I thought I was living the luxury life because my parents didn't have money like that to buy the things that I wanted. But they did make sure I had the things that I needed.

We both graduated high school in 1995. I moved to Brooklyn, New York where I attended Kings Borough Community College. I would still go back to Massachusetts to go visit my family and would meet up with him and hang out. At that point, we were sexually active. I remember I would always have to have a drink and get because I knew that was the only way for me to be sexually active with him. I ended up getting pregnant by him while I was in college. Even till this day I still don't know how that happened when we used a condom. I told him, and he was so happy. I brought it to his attention that I was two months pregnant and I was not planning on keeping the baby. Right, when I told him about my decision, the next morning he decided to take the Greyhound bus to Brooklyn to let my grandmother and family know about my pregnancy and what my intentions were. He was aware that my family would be against my decision. At this time, I was an eighteen-year-old college girl. What did I know about having a child when my focus was to finish college and be successful in life? My grandmother and family were so against me having an abortion to the point I ended up dropping out of college and keeping my pregnancy.

I was young, pregnant and trying to make things work with a man I knew I didn't love, and I didn't want to be with. Because of my family beliefs, I tried to make it work but deep down inside, I was angry at myself for getting pregnant by a man I did not want to be in a relationship with.

One day, when I was four months pregnant, Mr. Child Support Man began dragging me by my hair from his parent's third floor home in the projects, all the way outside where he kept beating me. Neighbors were standing around watching him beat me and did nothing to help. It took an old lady to come out her house with a broom to hit him with it just so he would stop beating on me. The police and ambulance came and rushed me to the hospital. The ER

Doctors couldn't hear my baby's heartbeat at first. I was scared and terrified that my baby was dead inside of me. Once I finally calmed down, the Doctor checked again and heard not only one heart beat but two heartbeats. God answered my prayers and saved my babies from leaving their mother's womb. He ended up getting arrested but was released the next day. Both his family and my family talked to me about not pressing charges and convinced me that I need my children's father to be there to help me with our babies. I listened to both side of the family and did not go through with the charges. But, the State ended up picking up the case but, because I refused to testify.

The case was dropped. My babies were born. A twin girl and boy, name Jazmyne Williana and Jameel Williamson Charles-Balan. I named their middle names after my father William, and my deceased brother Williamson, and my now deceased grandmother. He was mad that I didn't name our children after his mother and that I didn't give our children just his last name. This was a man that made my life a living hell for the next nineteen years of my Kids lives all because I did not want to be with him anymore. He would call the Department of Social Services and lie saying that I was neglecting and abusing my children just so they can take my children away because he refused to pay his little $69 or $80 for two children.

He would even go to the Probate court to file motions against me stating that I was neglecting my children and he shouldn't have to pay me child support. He even tried to turn my children against me by manipulating them into going to live with him so he wouldn't have to pay his child support. There was a time when he tried to team up with Mr.

Auction's baby mother to say that Mr. Auction had guns and drugs in my house. Mind you my Kids were twelve years old at the time. Department of Social Services came to investigate my home and asked me if I would take a drug test. I did just as they asked and passed the drug test. Imagine, your Kids being in school and strangers are coming there to question them about their well-being and the mother that's been taking care of them since being in her womb.

This man watched me, and his children live in a shelter, and still took me to court for $69 or $80 for two children all because I chose not to be with him. I would be in court blind in one eye, fighting over child support money.

I moved to Atlanta after Christmas in 2015. My children were living in college dorms, and I would go back to Boston every month to check up on them. Let me tell you what this man did. He waited until I moved to Atlanta and then decided to file a motion for dismissal of child support because he claimed that I emancipated them. At the time, the twins were nineteen years old, living in college dorms, paying for their school, and their financial aid was in my name.

When I went to court to answer his false accusations, he had gone to my Facebook page and took screen shots of pictures of me living in Atlanta for proof that the children did not live with me. I told the judge that I was throwing in the flag. I was just sick and tired of living my life in a courtroom. I told the judge to let him keep his $139 per week for his two teenage children. No amount of money will continue to affect my physical and emotional wellbeing. We had been going to court for nineteen years, and I was just tired. I took care of my children all by myself without his help and not once has he taken his children to a doctor's appointment or dentist appointment. He's never been to parent-teacher meetings but, made sure he was at their graduation to praise their achievements that he did not contribute to. My children are now old enough to know about the sacrifices that were made to ensure they had a decent life to be successful.

Mr. Chef: I met Mr. Chef at a lounge where we were watching a football game with mutual friends. We hit it off right off the bat. Mr. Chef worked as a cook for a short time and was a retired veteran. He fought in World War 2. When we met, he was working for the New York City Transit Department of Transportation. I must say the physical attraction was definitely there, and we quickly fell in love with each other. He was eleven years older than me. I met him when I was twenty-five, and he was thirty-six, and my twins were four years old at the time.

Within a year of our relationship, I ended up pregnant with my daughter Kiara. He did not want me to have my daughter. He even took me to the hospital to get an abortion. I pretended to be OK with the plan. But, I went to see the doctor for some pain that I was having in my lower abdomen. I made sure he didn't come in the patient's room so he wouldn't find out that I was not getting an abortion. I knew after having my twins, there was no way I was going to abort my unborn child. We left the hospital, and he asked me how I was feeling, and I told him I was fine. He took me out to eat for dinner and began apologizing for making me get an abortion. I played along and said to him no worries. After he had thought that I had gone through with the abortion, he went back to being the loving man that I fell in love with and things were back to normal.

I knew I couldn't keep the secret from him any longer. I waited until I started my second trimester and finally told him the truth. One evening, he took me out to eat and on our way back from dinner while he was driving me back home, I told him the truth. He stopped the car in the middle of the street, forcing me to get out of his car. I was holding on to the door while he was driving off with me holding on to the car and I fell in the middle of the street. I got myself up with the help of a stranger.

As time went by and he realized that I was going to keep the baby, he started to come around and doing what he was supposed to be doing. He knew I grew up in a family that believed in family values and morals. So, he started to do the right thing. We got a one bedroom apartment in Brooklyn for $1150 a month with no utilities included. My twins slept on the pull-out couch with us, and our newborn daughter slept in her crib in our room. I went back to work in six weeks following the birth of our daughter. We both were working but, he was having financial difficulties paying his half of the rent and utilities. At the time, I knew he had one son who was six years old by another woman. I began asking questions trying to find out why he was having such a difficult time taking care of his contributions towards the bills. He finally told me that his baby mother took him to court for child support and he needed to get a second job. Our lease was coming up for renewal, and I suggested to him that we could go to Boston and stay with my parents until we were able to get our own place where we both can manage the bills.

We stayed with my parents for one year while we both

worked and until I was able to buy us an eight-bedroom house in Springfield, Massachusetts. My Dad came and stayed with us for a while to help with remodeling. I was pregnant and ready to give birth in two months to our second child, a baby boy. I went into labor had our baby boy two months early. I delivered him at Massachusetts General Hospital in Boston, MA which was an hour and a half from our new home. Our baby boy came home to our new house and started to get sick and began wheezing. We were back and forth from Springfield to Boston with the baby. I ended up staying at my parents' house so that I would be closer to his medical doctor while our new home was being renovated and remodeled. When the city of Springfield came to inspect the house, they found that our home had carbon monoxide in it. The inspector said it was too dangerous for us to live there until the issue was resolved. Finally, we got the ok to come back to the house. He was working while stayed home to take care of a two-year-old, a Newborn, and two six-year-old twins. He was working two jobs and still not able to contribute to the bills.

I started my own private investigation by going through his things. I came across pay stubs with four different types of payments of child support coming out of his paycheck. I just couldn't figure out how a man can work two full- time jobs and still can't pay the bills in the house. Come to find out, he had three daughters by three different women living in the state of Georgia that he never told me about. The whole time I thought he was only paying child support for one child; his son. Nope! He had three daughters that he was also paying for, and this was the reason why he couldn't help with the bills around the house. I waited until he came home and brought it to his attention. He got so upset that he started to choke and punch me. I waited until he was at work and then packed my Kids and my clothes and took off to my parents' house. A month went by, and he realized that I was not coming back. He went to my parents' house begging me to forgive him and to try and work things out. I told him I was not going back there with him. So, he ended up staying with us at my parents' house. While at my parents' house, He couldn't even give them $50 a month for water bills or nothing. We still had a mortgage to pay and four Kids to take care of.

I started showing my frustration. I would not be as intimate with him as I used to. I began to do my own thing and act like he did not even exist. I woke up one day and told him he had to go back to Brooklyn. He started to beat me up in the house. I ran outside, and he ran after me continuing to beat me. A neighbor saw him beating the hell out of me and said he was going to call the police if he didn't stop. So, he called the police and said I was beating on him. The two officers came and began to question us as to what happened. I decided to look out for him by not saying he was beating me, but he told the officers that I was beating him. They arrested me, and when I got back home to my parent's house, he took off back to Brooklyn.

Later on that night, he called me to see how I was doing and to apologize. I told him to go to hell. He did not show up in court, so Charges were dropped against me. This man plays no part in our Kids lives. It's been years since he last contacted his two children. He never calls his children on holidays, or birthdays to wish them a Happy Birthday. Our son was diagnosed with Post Traumatic Stress Disorder from witnessing his father beat me up all the time. He was put in a behavioral school and on an I. E.P. Plan because he had so much anger inside of him because of what he had witnessed inside our home. It's sad a man can help create children and not be a part of his children's daily lives. But, that still will not stop me from being the best mother I know how to be for my children. Unbroken, Still I Smile.

Mr. Auction: I met Mr. Auction at my 31st Birthday party at a Bar and Grill in Lynn, MA. He was very persistent in trying to get my number, so we exchanged numbers. After I had left the Bar and Grille, my girlfriends and I went to an after party at a mutual friend's house. I had no idea Mr. Auction would be there, but sure enough, he came in and asked me to dance. It was my birthday, I had a few drinks in my system, and I was feeling myself. I danced the night away with him until the party was over, then we both went our separate ways.

The next day he called me. We talked on the phone for hours nonstop for the next few days getting to know each other. Throughout our conversation, I talked about my children, and he told me that he had one child but did not disclose who his baby mother was. A friend of mine called and told me who the baby mother was and to stay away from him because he was trouble and his baby mother was ghetto and ratchet. She also said that he was pimping prostitutes for money. Once I found out who his baby's mother was, I was speechless! I see why he didn't want to tell me her name. It made a lot of sense because this woman had a bad reputation in our community. I knew her from growing up and had mutual friends but, we never had each other's numbers or hung out. When I brought it to his attention, he told me he knew if he had told me too soon that I wouldn't give him a chance to talk to me. He admitted that he was aware that she had a bad reputation but, she was a good mother to his son. He also mentioned his past mistakes and how he was a changed man. I respected him for saying that she was a good mother with regardless of how she is on the streets. He begged me to give him a chance, so I did.

The more time we spent together. The closer we became. It was obvious that he wasn't raised with the same family values or morals as me. But, you could tell he was very excited about being with a girl who already had her life together. At the same time, I always felt that he was in it for what I could give and offer him.

I was driving a Hummer when I first met him. At that time, he didn't have a car but had a motorcycle. That's when I should've really used my brain. You work at an auction, have a motorcycle but, not a car? But, I was falling for him. I felt that he was a good person but, loved to front for his friends and the streets. He wanted to change his life but, was still trapped in the loyal street life.

A month went by, and I began to get threatening phone calls from his baby mother letting me know that she did not want me around their son. Mind you, she never had an issue with me before. All of a sudden, I started getting threatening calls from her saying that she would kick my ass if she finds out her son has been around me. I told her that my relationship is not with you, it's with your son's father. If your son's father feels like I'm not good enough to be around your child, he will be the one to tell me. After that, I asked her nicely not to call or make a threat to me again. And from there, the real drama begins.

Mr. Auction told me not to pay her any attention and that she was just jealous of me. I told Mr. Auction that I was too old for all the drama, especially, with a man that I don't even have children with. I was not going to mess up my career by going to jail for beating up his baby mother. I went to court and was granted a restraining order for her to stay away and to not contact me. We decided to move in together and make it official and commit ourselves to each other. Oh, boy was that a big mistake. Mr. Auction got served with child support papers although he had been faithfully taking care of their son, who was five years old at the time. We faithfully had him every weekend. But the one time, we decided to go to a concert to enjoy some quality time. I was getting texts from his baby mother telling me to tell Mr. Auction that she was dropping their son off. I told her it had nothing to do with me and that she needed to speak to her baby father about arrangements for their son. I passed him the message about her blowing up my phone and leaving random text messages. As we arrived at the parking lot where the show was being held, Mr. Auction and I were getting out of the car, and a female screams his name, starts talking and yelling all kinds of derogatory words. He told me to keep walking, and that he would meet me at the door because he was going to speak with her.

We finally go inside to meet his friends and their significant others. We were having a really good time and enjoying the show when all of a sudden someone came, and sucker punched me in the back of my head. I was hysterically fighting a woman, whom I've never met in my entire life. All I knew was that I was fighting back and defending myself. Mr. Auction and his friends broke up the fight. Come to find out, it was his baby mother's entourage that sucker punched me from behind.

When I returned home, I packed his clothes in trash bags, threw them outside, and told him that I was done with this nonsense, and we were finished. I was so heated. I felt very violated and disrespected. When their son was at our house, I was the one making sure he was fed, showered, bought him clothes, and taking him on family trips just to make sure he was comfortable in our presence. I would take him along with us to my children's activities while he would be at home sleeping. So, this time I'm back at Lynn court for a restraining against the baby mothers friend. Now the baby mother decided to go to Salem Superior Court to get a restraining order against me because I got one against her friend for sucker punching me from behind. The judged denied her the restraining order because he saw that she was acting out of jealousy and ended up putting the restraining order against her enforcing her to not get out her car when she drops her son off to Mr. Auction.

Because of this, she decides to keep him from seeing his son. This just added more stress and drinking to Mr. Auction. He started coming home drunk, taking his anger and frustration out on me. He would slap me, bang my head and push me against the wall for no reason. The next morning, he wouldn't even remember what he did to me the night before. It kept escalating more and more until I ended up in the Emergency room for fractured arms. I lied to the Doctors and Nurses by telling them that I fell down my stair. He was sitting right next to me on the hospital bed, and I was lying for him.

I tried leaving him numerous times. But every time I

tried to leave, he would take my bottle of pills and try to swallow them, attempting suicide. That would make me change my mind about leaving because I was terrified that he would try to kill himself and it would be my fault. I found out from his mother that he tried to take his life in the past and that he had been molested by a family member at a young age.

Now it all makes sense as to why he would always be fighting in his sleep. His mother was in and out of his life. He grew up without a father. All he knew was the street life and how to be loyal to the streets. As time went on and I began to see for myself everything that my friend was telling me in the beginning. She was right! I went downstairs to my living room and found a prostitute laying on my couch. I went crazy and told him that she needed to get out of my house right now! He said that she didn't have to leave because he pays rent too. A share of $625 that he could never pay on time because he was out there spending and splurging in the streets.

We rented a room to his friend but, that was a mistake. They used the room as a hangout and smoking room which was right next door to my son's room who had asthma. He didn't even care about my kid's health, had no respect for my children or me. We had a basement. Why not just use the basement to smoke?

There were times when I would let my kids stay at my parents' house because I didn't want them to be around that type of environment. It was one thing after another. His baby mother getting a hold of my twin's father, telling him her baby father is no good for me and that he has guns and drugs in my house. The department of Social Services were investigating my home, and asked me to take a drug test. They were at my children's school questioning them and their teachers, verifying with their Doctors to make sure they were up to date and making sure the doctors hadn't noticed any neglect or physical abuse. We were constantly arguing, and he was constantly beating the hell out of me! Back to the emergency room, I go again! I was getting my head hit against the walls, which caused me to have severe migraines and an anxiety attack. And as usual, he was sitting right next to me in the emergency room, and I was lying for him.

When we got back home, he said that he was sorry and things were back to normal again. When Friday came around, he went out splurging his check at the club instead of paying bills. The next morning, I found lipstick and sunglasses that didn't belong to me. Whenever he goes to take a shower, he takes his phone in the bathroom with him.

I knew something wasn't right with him. I started to observe and began to care less about what he did. I got to a point where I started to have numerous anxiety attacks from stressing out and overthinking about what my next move was going to be. I knew I was tired of being taken for granted, being hurt, used, abused, as well as maintaining 90% of the household bills. I cut my hours at work to part time. I focused on my schooling and graduated with my second college bachelor's degree. I knew I wasn't going to stay with him. I had a plan. I pretended to be broke to him while I was saving my money for two years. He thought that I was still working the same part-time job but, I had a full-time job and continued to stack my money.

Since he wanted to have females in my Hummer that I put $10,000 down on, I made him pay the car note which was $418 a month, and the car insurance which was $278. I told him it was $520. I saved the difference in another bank account that I opened separately.

The very last time he beat me up was when he came home drunk. He wanted to have sex with me. I told him no! He pushed me off the bed, and I fell on the floor. I was fed up. I got up and began to defend myself. I remember running out of the bedroom. He followed me to the living room and started kicking me and banging my head on the floor while choking me until I fell unconscious. When I opened my eyes, he was holding me saying I'm sorry. I pretended to forgive him and said that everything was going to be ok like always. I told him that I was going to check on the kids. When I went to their room, my two youngest were in the corner of their room scared. I called my girlfriend and was crying to her on the phone telling her what had just happened. She said I'm on my way to get you. A few minutes went by, and the doorbell rang. I opened the door, and it was the police. They asked to come in and asked me if I was ok. One officer took me into the kitchen to speak to me while the other officer was flashing the light in his face to wake him up because he had passed out on the couch dead drunk. I told the officer that I was okay. He said you know I can't help you if I don't know what exactly happened. My dress was ripped. The officer asked me what happened to my dress and why I had a hand print around my neck. I told the officer I got into a fight with a girl earlier that day. But, he knew that I was lying. After the officers had left, he took my cell phone and threw it outside in the middle of the Main Street.

An hour later, my girlfriend came to pick my children and me up. We dropped the kids off to my parents, then she drove me to the police station where we ran into the same two police officers that were at my house. I broke down and cried saying, I can't do this anymore! They called the ambulance for me and went back to my house to arrest him. It happened the Saturday of Memorial Day weekend, so that meant he wasn't going in front of the judge until Tuesday. His mother called me and asked me what had happened. I told her the exact truth of what happened. Her exact words to me were, "I don't care if he's my son, never let a man puts his hands on you." But, Tuesday morning came, and it was time for court. I went in there, and his mom and her daughter didn't say anything to me. It was from there I knew what time it was with them. I even got in front of the judge and lied for him saying that he didn't do it. The judge told me "ma'am you need to talk to legal services because I don't think you know what you're doing. If you are lying, you can be found guilty of perjury. You can do two and half years in jail. The lawyer explained to me the law and suggested that I plead the fifth. While I sat in court listening to the district attorney read his rap sheet, I was speechless. This was a man that committed a lot of crimes such as intimating witnesses, gang related, and the list goes on and on. They had him listed as a danger to society.

After leaving the court, I was at a stop sign in my truck. Out of nowhere comes his sister reaching into my car, swinging at me. Needless to say, she got arrested. I decided not to go through with pressing charges. I was scared that he would come after my family or me. I even went to bail him out for $2500. When I arrived, the bondman was gone for the day and would not be back until the next morning. He had to go to work, so his boss sent one of his co-workers to bail him out.

Even after he got out, he called me crying and apologizing. I still took him back. Now he needed me more than ever but, there was still fear that he might do something to my family. Imagine hearing a judge reading a four-page rap sheet about the man you thought you knew and loved. You would become cautious making sure that he didn't go after your family members too. Especially when he has been known for duct taping people down in basements. I feared for my family. But I took him back again, except now we were living in separate locations.

He would come over my house and stay for the weekends. He even went through the trouble of putting $6000 down on a nice Mercedes-Benz R350, just to shut me up so that I wouldn't testify against him. The remaining balance on the Hummer was only $2800. Mind you both cars were in my name, registered and insured. I let him drive the Hummer because I was driving the Benz. But, when my eight-year-old son finds you passed out in the Hummer with the key in the ignition, in our driveway all night, then there's a problem. I'm not going to jail if you end up hurting or killing someone because you decided to drive drunk. I went and paid the balance on the Hummer and got my title. I knew at that moment that I had reached my breaking point with his madness. But, when I knew for sure was when I woke up on August 31, 2013. I had lost the vision in my right eye due to being diagnosed with Multiple Sclerosis. He didn't spend not one night with me in the hospital aside from coming to see me for 45 minutes with one of his male friends. And to think, I kept him out of jail and played the role of his mother rather than a girlfriend.

There were times when he would come home at 4am smelling like sex every weekend. And to top it all off, he got a young Hispanic girl from Lowell, Massachusetts pregnant, and made her get an abortion.

I put up with so much dealing with his trash that it has made me stronger and taught me not to deal with trash anymore. All the kicks, head banging on the floor and walls, throwing me out of the car and throwing a plate of food at me in the middle of a Main Street, using and abusing me, telling me that no other man would put up with my bullshit and take me with my four kids. Me, pretending like my hours were reduced and pretending to be broke just so that he hopefully would stop splurging at the bars and coming home with empty pockets. I let him walk free. All the while I knew that deep down inside in my heart that I was going to turn all the negatives into a positive situation because now I am "Unbroken, Still I Smile."

Overcoming domestic violence takes a will of courage, strength, hope and faith. I thank God for instilling in me each and every one of those traits. I overcame domestic violence when I got diagnosed with Multiple Sclerosis on August 31, 2013. I felt deep in my heart that it was God saying to me "if MS is not going to wake you up to leave your abusive relationship then I don't know what else will." I remember how I would talk to God and ask him to give me signs and help me to overcome the cycle of abuse. I asked him to give me strength and courage. He did just that. God doesn't give you anything you can't handle. Since I've left the abusive relationship, God has been opening doors for me left and right. He's replacing all the wrong people with the right ones. Trust in him! He knows what he's plans are for you.

You just have to believe in Him, have faith, and take the first step. Taking that first step shows that we trust God to take care of us.

I was sexually assaulted at the tender age of six years old. I experienced three awful, abusive relationships, and now living with MS, which was triggered by the last abusive relationship. These are the reasons why I am working so hard and steadfast at fulfilling all of my dreams and goals. I don't know if or when I'll end up wheelchair bound, but while I'm able to still walk on my own two feet, I want to empower women and let them know that they are not alone. There are resources out there that are ready to help you regain self-confidence and your dignity.

Believe in God and put him first in your life. I look at my children everyday day and know that they would be lost without their mother. I'm all that my children have. They've witness and experienced the struggle with me. I was both a mother and father figure to my children. The best love to any child is a mother's love. Do not let any man take you out of this world and allow your kids to grow up without a mother. How did I become a domestic violence survivor? My children, and living with Multiple Sclerosis gave me the strength to say enough was enough. God will lead you. But first, you have to show him that you're ready to be led by following his footsteps. I knew I deserved better than what I was getting.

I now know and understand that a real man who truly loves me, will not hurt me or abuse me. Know and understand that real love does not hurt! "Unbroken, Still I smile."

SURVIVOR TALK
Wisdom

God will use whatever he wants to display his glory.

A season of suffering is a small assignment when compared to the reward. Your problems, struggles, and pain all have a purpose. Rather than be angry about the things that you have gone through, explore it. Ponder it. Use it to the glory of God.

- What does the word "wisdom" mean to you?
- Explain how your life's experiences have shaped your views of wisdom?

Understand that the wounds of your reality were meant for a purpose. –Wisdom

Chapter Two

WHAT ABOUT US?
Domestic Violence - A Childs View
"If You See Something, Say Something"
By Venus Miller

The shell of what the life of a child is like when trauma hits. It's not just a lost life. It's children left motherless or fatherless or both. Who follows the children? Who helps them? If they are not helped the trauma can continue.

The day my life changed forever: I was just 5 years old and never could imagine that life would be so cold. The day that would change and infect my life. This day shaped my mind to experience a shocking dose of hurt, pain, fear, abandonment, and rejection at such an early age. This would force me to be fake and fight to survive. The night I REMEMBER was really like no other. It was me and my four brothers. This night I was not sure where my mother had gone. We were never alone. I would not understand until later in my life that because my mother left home without my father's permission, she lost her life. My daddy would come home on some days during the week and then the turmoil, the yelling, and the fear of my mother I know now would appear. My mother, a victim of domestic violence for many years, had experienced blackened eyes, broken limbs, and most of all, breaking of a total person, mentally, physically, emotionally and sexually. Her self-worth and self-esteem were so low, in despair and no hope that she no longer willed to live, I'm sure. Soon she would turn to alcohol and depression would soon follow. No family, friends and not even the law helped. Fear gripped her very soul and telling anyone was not an option. What about us?

The death of my mother: Well, this night I'm told my mother had gained enough boldness to leave and go to the tavern up the street. My mother left specific instructions with my oldest brother, "If your dad goes in our top drawer, call 911, there is a gun there, and he will kill me because he told me he would ". On this night, my father came home unexpected as he usually would and woke up my oldest brother to ask, "where is your mother?" my brother responded, "She went outside." My father went into the top drawer and hurried out the front door. My oldest brother would attempt to call 911, but as he has said many times, he dialed every number except 911. My oldest brother said that my father would find my mother at the bar up the street sitting next to a male stranger. Rage, jealousy, and anger so strong that my father would physically assault my mother from the tavern all the way to the front of our apartment complex. Shouting, screaming, assaulting and shooting at my mother as she ran screaming. My mother's last words were "Mack, Mack you shot me. The last bullet would travel through her hand to her heart and end her life on that day. I'm reminded that is was around Mother's Day. I remember being awoken early in the morning, cops and family at the door. Everyone was sad and crying. Your mother will not be coming back home. Huh? But why? What does that mean? What about us?

The longest limo ride - The funeral: My mommy is really dead! My mind is still blank until the ride in the limousine. I have on all white, and my brothers have on suits. We don't know what to really do or say. The ride seemed so long. I don't remember a lot of people being there. We walk in the funeral home, and I see a long white casket. Why I remember a glass being over her? I don't know, but it's lowered for us so we can see. I'm saying "mommy, mommy" but she will not talk to me. Why can't she get up and come home with us? Where is my daddy? All I remember was saying mommy, mommy why won't you answer me. Then it's over, and we are back in the limousine for a long ride back to grandma's house. Then we begin to cry, but immediately we are told to "shut up! It's over, and she is not coming back, and I can give you something to cry for". It was all of our first introduction to the nice but not so nice world of "FAMILY." I was young, but I understood what it meant to just be quiet. My dad would be sentenced to ten years in jail at this time. This is where life was, one incident after another as my brothers, and I learned to adapt and smile. Sadly, we still do not know where my mother is buried. My mother was half white and half black. Nobody helped back then, my mother was considered "white trash" by some. The broken arms and black eyes were ignored by all, and now that her life had come to this tragic end my family wanted it to just go away, so it was not discussed, avoided and ignored. We did not discuss it, we did not talk about her. We never memorialized her, and we did not properly grieve. It was forbidden to act sad. Why was asking about my mother so sad? Why could I not ask about my mommy? It hurt so bad! What about us? We were children! How could everyone just go on pretending that this was not a must! Lord, what about us?

My Childhood: The devastation continues - New York City. Separation began almost immediately. Who was going to be able to take care of all of us? It started with my mother's mom, but that ended quickly. My mother was an only child. My grandmother, distraught and I'm sure overwhelmed, would drink daily. One day she hit her head on the corner table at my parents' home and just like that, she too was gone! Again, my oldest brother could not dial 911. My poor brother. We would never see her again. Like my mother where she is buried would never be known. We moved with my father's parents. This included my father's father and step mother. They were nice but very vulgar, loud and cursed as it was normal. Strong discipline and respect were demanded. But their stature and presence would automatically make us understand it. There was no sexual abuse, but emotionally and mentally my family lacked sensitivity. I noticed the woman to be strong and tough, and I don't believe I ever saw tears. My step grandmother was the disciplinarian and what she said went. My grandfather although strong, did what she said to do. My oldest brother lived with us temporarily then would move with one of my aunts in Chicago. My next to the oldest brother would end up in foster care along with my youngest brother. Me and my brother under me would stay together throughout childhood up until this very day. My baby brother was the most concerning. My mother was an alcoholic, and domestic violence was constant during and after pregnancy. As a result, my brother was born underdeveloped, with a small brain, stunted stature, and needing constant medication resulting in a year of hospitalization before being released. My baby brother also ended up in foster care. We did get a chance to meet my uncles, cousins, and friends. The family had its own way of love. We gathered often, I went to a Catholic school, was taught manners and my family did show a level attention in certain areas. Academic excellence was important. We did do a lot of fun things, but I know that we were dysfunctional.

We lived the motto "whatever happens in the house stays in the house." I witnessed the drinking and marijuana on several occasions. I learned the silent, and "I don't see anything" game early. The truth is, nobody could love me enough because I simply wanted my mother. We would live here for a little while but for reasons unknown to me, my father's mother would send for us to come live in Miami. My oldest brother would remain with my aunt, and my other two brothers would stay in foster care. I did see my brothers on special occasions, but we never got a chance to grow together and build a child hood relationship. I would not see my brothers again until my teenage years. My family loved the way they loved which is unexplainable at best. Today I will tell you that they may have had guilty moments and expressed that not talking about my mother made them not think about what they could have done. I do understand now, but as I child all I could say was "what about us?"

My grandma's House - Miami Florida: The move to Miami was scary. My brother, and I were already trained to be quiet. I was still in shock about my mother and held it deep in my heart. I trained myself not to cry. I would start talking to God and mostly doing make believe pretending she was alive. When my friends would ask me where my mommy and daddy were, I would say" they are at work and can't come." At 8 years old, I developed an attitude of my own. I get to meet the other side of my father's family and even my mother's family. I meet my grandmother. This is where I was introduced to kindness, love, and discipline. She was not abusive. She loved God and never smoked, drank or cursed. WOW! What a change. I was in trouble mostly because I began to release some attitude with my mouth, but it was corrected. I learned a lot from my grandmother. She took us everywhere. We never felt threatened or afraid. We lived here for a few years and really functioned as children should. She taught me how to be a young lady and how to be respectful. I felt like I obtained a new family. My grandmother took us to church and shaped our minds to forgive and love GOD. She never spoke of my mother or father, and neither did I. My younger brother would always be there right next to me. He was quiet, observant and did what he was told. Then one night the dream ended! I was close to 10 years old. My grandfather, obviously drunk, came into my room. He took his hand and rubbed it up the crack of my back side with his thumb. It was dark, my brother on the other side of me in the green and yellow room with two beds. I would never forget. As an instinct of a woman, my grandmother got up as I began to scream noooo!!! She screamed no!!! Again, my life came to an immediate stop. I looked at my brother, tears in my eyes like I'm sorry I don't want to move! I won't say nothing! This is the nicest place we have been. By the morning my grandmother would say "it's time to go to your aunt's house. We all knew why? I couldn't even cry. I had so many mixed feelings. What about us? I did not see my grandfather for many years after that day. It would not be until after college that I would go back to stay. Why? I really wanted to stay.

My Aunts House. Next stop: My aunt has eight older children. Six boys, and two girls. Again, the incident at my grandmothers was not discussed. We were crowded in a house full of strange love again. My aunt was divorced but had a live-in boyfriend. She was also the disciplinarian with an alcoholic problem. When she drank she was nice, cooked a lot of food, we played cards, sang songs, and talked surprisingly about my mother. She would cry every time she talked about it. She was my father's sister, and she did not condone what my father did. She would say "somebody should have helped my mother." She would say "I don't know what got into my brother." She would tell me "you look just like your mother." Then the next day would come, and the anger would happen. Cleaning the house, screaming, washing all the clothes and very cranky. Amazing, the difference one day would make. My brother and I would deal with the mood swings. After a while, we learned what not to do. My cousins, what an experience of confusion. At this time, I was getting older, and my body is growing. A house full of children and the games begin. The problem would come from her oldest son. Physical violation started very subtle. I knew something was wrong but didn't know what to say or do. The experience would go from peaking in the bathroom to touching in the middle of the night, to awakening to a body on top of mine to a penis in my mouth tasting like salt. At first, I was in simple disbelief. He would offer me candy and chips and try to be nice when we were playing, but I would always feel sick to my stomach. I was too scared to tell anyone. This would go on from the age of 10-16.

One day I got the nerve to write my aunt a note. The response would be "you must have liked it because you took so long to tell me." BOOM!! What? I was crushed. My father was now out of jail, and we would be shipped back to my father in New York City. Sworn to never speak of anything that had happened, because my family knew my father's rage. I would keep that secret for another 20 years. This would shape my actions, my tolerance, my temperament and my attitude. By now I had enough. I was older now. I entered New York with my mind set that nobody would hurt me again and to trust no one. What about us?

I meet my father again, and at first, he is very nice, but soon we are back to when I was 5. The domestic violence is continuing, and he has beaten his new wife several times. She had been with him for several years. My father and I had several verbal and one physical altercation. He slapped me for talking back so hard that the vision in my right eye remains poor. I remember urinating on myself that day. I told him I hated him and I'm not afraid of him like my mother, and everyone else was. He threatened to throw me off the 22nd-floor balcony. I kindly responded it will be two of us. My father never threatened me again. My father was stern and lacked love for my younger brother, and he eventually went to live with my aunt. I was not allowed to go to parties or go to my Prom. I reconnected with my 2 older brothers very briefly. They were in the army and navy but at this point, they were physically assaulting their wives. My father and my two brothers would end up divorced and alone. My younger brother under me would also go on to be in the military and do very well. With violence never a part of him, he is now a pastor and we currently attend the same church. He has been married over 25 years, which is amazing for our family. My father has since passed away. It was a long struggle, but forgiveness did take place. He was a great grandfather, and my kids didn't know anything until recently. My oldest brother is remarried, remains an alcoholic and still blames himself for my mother's death. My second oldest brother was an alcoholic for many years. This was due to hurt, anger and bitterness concerning foster care. He has recovered for over 5 years and on his 3rd degree. Currently reconciling with his children after 20 years.

My baby brother lives around the corner and is doing well

after many setbacks. The cousin that molested me as a young girl went to jail for molesting others and died by drowning a year ago. What about us?

Once I left for college, I never would return back home. I struggled through college. Got in several poor relationships. Failed out of my first nursing school after getting pregnant and having an abortion. I would move back to Miami with my grandmother without incident. I successfully completed my nursing degree at Barry University in 1990 pregnant with my first son. Failed my first nursing boards. Delivered my son 2 weeks after graduation and retook my boards and passed them and got married for the first time.

My marriage seemed awesome. I got married in the church where my grandmother raised me. Sadly I would suffer a heart break while carrying my second child. My husband was having an affair with my friend, the godmother of my children and a participant in my wedding. We were pregnant at the same time. She would later get an abortion. The news so devastating that I would have a mental breakdown, suffer from depression and become suicidal. This is when all the hurt from my past would resurface. I suffered from great depression but because I was taught early how to be fake, I would go to work and smile, come home and cry, put my kids to bed and plan to kill them and myself. God said, "you will live and not die:" how? What do you want God? You took my mother, my father, my brothers and my husband? I divorced my first husband with a vengeance!

The next marriage: I met my next husband while still married. I told my soon to be ex-husband "it's over," I'm seeing someone else. Within 2 weeks, I moved him in. We both went through a divorce and got married. We would be married for 10 years. I would become the first lady. I could speak the word, minister but I could also be mean, loud, and nasty. Nobody could tell me anything. We argued often. I pretended often. Deep down I was still angry, hurt, betrayed, rejected and alone. I had not healed yet. I had no business being married. I returned back to school for another degree, but I still did not feel better. After a while, I no longer wanted to go to church. I would meet another male friend who wanted to just talk and have fun. And the affair began. Did I know I was? I was so broken? Not validated? Unforgiving? Suspicious? If you made one mistake, I was leaving? Again, one day I walked in to tell my husband I was divorcing him. I packed up my children and abandon that house to start life again. What about us? What about me?

The turmoil and the affair: After the divorce, I was free again! Who would tell me anything? I would be like this for 10 years. From being the first lady at church, to being in the club, hanging out, doing what I want, no church, just work. I could care less. Met a married man and had an affair for 5 long years. One day his wife would call. It was as if a light went off. My daughter would say mom come to church. Noooooo way. I was alone again, depressed, anxious, isolated, but I again went for one more degree. This always helped me. I obtained my 2nd masters in Psychiatry. I did not realize how infected I was. I needed help. I went back to church. Ended the affair. Got professional help. Asked my kids for forgiveness. I was honest with my children and family. God dealt with me, and I began to speak to my father again.

Forgiveness: After I forgave myself and others. I began to share my story and realized I was not alone. "Time to talk for real" Most people talk about domestic violence survivorship.

But what about the children of the violence? Did not anyone understand that they need help too? Do you know what it's like to never have your mother or father and to be handed to this evil world? Do you know why they repeat the behavior like my brothers did? Hurt others, infect others, and turn to drugs, mentally tormented, promiscuous, low self-esteem or an arrogant phony over achiever. All trying to find a love they will never have. So, I always say, don't stay in a domestic violence relationship for your children! Get out for your children, because the long-term effects of trauma and abuse grows with the child, and if they don't get help, they will hurt themselves and others too.

Meeting my dream: After it was all said and done, I met someone. Me? Married? Oh no. this man began to pray and speak life to me, and he is my husband today. I speak to all those I give my testimony to, about starting over, forgiveness and the process of healing. Hurt people hurt people but healed people heal people. I had to deal with the issues in my mind, stop being phony, expose the truth, and let it go! Now my worth! Accept my purpose and embrace my call. Today I can say it was worth it all. I am healed, and my mission is to help others be real and accept the life they have been given, forgive and live. This is why it's important to know about your children "what about us? What about the children". Don't let them get hurt. Don't turn your head! "If you see something say something." Kids grow up too! What did we allow to infect them? We should be aware, because that same child can grow to infect another and the cycle will continue!! STOP THE VIOLENCE NOW!!!

Today I am happy to be transparent! To tell the truth! I will be the voice of the child! I remember back then, but today

I WIN! CERTIFIED FAMILY & PSYCHIATRIC NURSE
PRACTITIONER.

SURVIVOR TALK
Affirmations of Peace

Now more than ever, we want to maintain inner peace no matter what is going on around us. Therefore, we should not let fear control our lives.

Peace embraces me today

I deserve to be peaceful

With every breath, I become more peaceful

Peace surrounds me in everything that I do

The more love and peace I extend, the more I receive it

I deserve a peaceful life now

I feel peaceful and joyful

I create peace and harmony for myself

I accept peace into every facet of my existence

I choose to live a peaceful life today

I breathe in peace

I allow peace to penetrate every cell of my being

Not All Wounds Are Visible.
~Wounds to Wisdom

Chapter Three

PRISONER OF LOVE
By Dr. Yamma Brown Alexander

*The ultimate measure of a man is not where
he stands in moments of comfort and
convenience, but where he stands in time
of challenge and controversy.*
--Dr. Martin Luther King Jr.

Our first house was in a ritzy residential area of Augusta, on a street called Walton Way. Our neighbors were Augusta's aristocracy: doctors and lawyers and other high-powered professionals. You could hardly miss us. We were the only African-American family, and we had a pony in the backyard. At Christmastime, the glowing, blinking black Santa Claus on the front lawn gave us away. Dad had our animated Santa custom-made along with Uncle Sam and Frosty the Snowman and a host of other illuminated cartoon figures. Every year, a new character popped up. And every year, from Thanksgiving to New Year's Day, curiosity seekers came from all over to see our Christmas pageant. I remember peeking out from behind our heavy living room curtains and seeing cars creeping past our house, most of them stopping just long enough for the people to ogle inside and the twinkling, jerking display of a few photographers before driving off. I'm not sure if they came for the decorations of for a glimpse of James Brown changing a dead bulb or righting a leaning lawn ornament. It was probably a little of both. YES! My dad was the late James

Brown, and you just got a glimpse into what life was like growing up BROWN.

My life wouldn't always be a fairy tale, so that's why I start the story there. At age 10 my life took a tremendous turn as a lot of families do. It started with a separation then later a divorce of my parent's. I knew there had been arguments, BOY had there been arguments and beatings. More than I saw I am sure. I didn't know that wasn't normal, all I knew is that it was over. MY mom finally said NO MORE, and that was when my life changed. I didn't stop being the daughter of a legend, and thankfully I was still allowed to be in my father's life. I say allowed because even with all his flaws he wanted to be there. That means a lot because there are a lot of father's that won't step up to that responsibility. I still could experience from time to time the luxurious lifestyle and fame that goes along with being an icon. There was also the Baltimore raised girl that lived in a middle-class neighborhood and had "regular" teenage fun. Growing up riding bikes, playing outside, going to the mall or skating rink. I excelled in school but even with all that I knew in my heart there was a huge part of me way down in South Carolina, and I always felt that connection.

When I met my future husband, I was working clinical rotations at Dekalb Medical Center in Atlanta and was the clinical pharmacist on the medical team taking care of his stepfather. You couldn't miss Darren, he was a bear of a man at six feet 3 inches tall and 250 pounds. He was also charismatic and smart. And he was a real flirt. "Oh, you look so cute in your lab coat!" he'd say. "Please don't tell me you have a boyfriend!" At first, I stuck to conversations about his stepfather's meds. But the more he talked, the more interested I became in him. He said he was an investment banker of an international company and that he had played baseball for the New York Mets. He was well educated, and honor student who had earned his undergraduate degree at Loyola University in New Orleans and pledged Kappa Alpha Psi at Tulane. When he asked me to dinner, I accepted. That was February 1998. I didn't tell Darren who my father was. Not at first, I didn't need another person using me for my namesake. A couple of months into the relationship, when I finally did fess up. Darren acted like he had no idea my father was James Brown.

I fell in love with the idea of Darren. What he represented on paper. Sure, he had some physical qualities that I loved, athletic and tall. He was also someone that studied a lot, about different things. He was well versed, and that was attractive to me because it was familiar. I had traveled the world at a young age and been exposed to so many different people, cultures, and lifestyles. I felt that anyone I was going to be with HAD to have those qualities. Hence, my "list" of acceptable qualities in a boyfriend. I had so much to learn, but I digress. My father had planted in me that my future husband had to give me what he did and I believed that. There were times when I knew that was impossible, but I loved the idea of someone giving me back what I had in my childhood. I was willing to get those things at all costs, and that attitude is what kept me in chained to an unrealistic and dangerous lifestyle.

Things between Darren and I moved fast after that. After dating for only 2 months, we visited Dad in Beech Island, SC. To my complete surprise, Darren asked my Dad for my hand I marriage. I almost spit my drink out! It was a scene from Coming to America. This was before he even asked me! I thought it was a bit old fashioned but sweet. Dad was impressed by Darren's success. I think he was just relieved that I wasn't with someone trying to smooch off of me an only interested in my bank account. Let me paint this picture for

you. As little girls, sometimes you believe in fairy tales. You believe your Prince Charming will come in on that white horse and that HE is the one. I felt like the LUCKY one. I felt like one day I would be the queen of a castle. Well, not literally but you know what I mean. So, needless to say I was swept up in his web and there was no looking back. I saw my dad happy with my choice. "If you're happy then I'm happy," Dad said. A month later I was formally engaged. 3 months after being together we were pledging to be husband and wife. It happened on Mother's Day, Darren and I were celebrating Mother's Day with our family, and he dropped down on one knee and asked. He said, "I can't imagine life without anyone but you." Everyone was shocked including me. I hadn't expected it, but Darren loved surprises.

Living with someone is quite different from dating them. I quickly learned Darren was jealous when he would tense up if I said high to the doorman at the elevator or came home a few minutes late. One day I planned to go shopping for some new things for our place, and Darren was convinced I was going to meet a man. I was like, NO I am going shopping for our place. He started arguing with me about leaving the apartment. I was stunned by his belligerence. I only wanted to go shopping, what is up with this dude!? He was convinced otherwise. I could not reason with him, so I grabbed my car keys and walked away. I figured he must be stressed, he needed to cool off. He followed me into the elevator and down to my car in the garage. He was pointing his finger up in my face and calling me stupid. I was a bit scared and was like I need to just get away for him. He wouldn't let up. He was calling me a bitch, slut, and whore for wanting to go out. As soon as I got to my car and got my keys out, he slammed them to the pavement. When I tried to pick them up, he pushed me back down to the ground. He did that about 3 or 4 four times until I almost broke my ankle in my heels. So, I took them off and started WALKING. I said surely, he won't follow me. He will probably pick up the key's and go in the house. Absolutely not! He FOLLOWED me down the side walk and down the street. Are you really doing this right now!? I screamed! "What is wrong with you!? I have never seen you like this", I said. By this time, I was walking back up the street toward our high-rise building to go in the front and ask a security guard to call the police. No, I didn't have a phone in my hand, remember my purse and keys were slapped down with everything I had. He followed me, and when we got there I just stayed with the security officers for a while, and he went up to the apartment. I said I am not going up there but never called the cops. He left after about 15-20 minutes and told the security officers I could go up and he would leave. I went back up into our 2-bedroom apartment, took a shower and laid down. I had slept for hours and didn't hear from him. I was worn out, a little sore from some bruises but still looked for him. He was there in our second bedroom sleep. So, I went back to our bedroom and went to sleep. Why didn't I run? I could have left then. I know then I wanted to tough it out. I had convinced myself he was stressed, and that's exactly what he said the next morning. I finally woke up to the smell of food and flowers, followed by a big apology. The apologies and the promises always come after the abuse. I learned year's later it's the way an abusive person copes with their abusive behavior.

I finally left after a night of terror. I had come home to our house on Tuxedo Rd in Buckhead in Atlanta, GA. Our neighbors were some of the most influential in the city. We were the YOUNGEST couple in the neighborhood, and one of the very few black couples there. If someone were leaving a package at the door, they would say I am looking for the owners. I would wave and say, yes, that's me. Ooh! With an awkward look on their face. One day one of the neighbor's kids came over and asked is your husband, Tyler Perry!? What, no! I said. Nothing against Tyler, I just couldn't understand the absurdity. I know kids will be kids, so I wasn't upset with them but where are your parents. It took some getting used to the neighborhood. By the time this incident happened, I was truly a Buckhead Becky, and a little Baltimore hood still left in me to know some shit was about to pop off at my house.

I immediately saw that Darren had been drinking. Little did I know it was for most of the day. He wanted to know why I was getting in so late, which it wasn't. It may have been 9 or 10pm. It didn't matter to him. He wanted to talk about my Dad's business and if I had convinced my family to let him manage the estate. I said, "Look, I am not the only person in the estate!" He snapped, "But you and your sister have the most influence!" He knew we were close to our dad and the people around him so we could make all the decisions because we were his children. In a perfect world, it works that way, except when millions are at stake.

That night 2 people went to the ER, the ambulance showed up at our home to check me out. Several of Atlanta PD was there, and our formal living room looked like a crime scene. I was being checked for a concussion. It was the worst night I had ever been through, and it involved my HUSBAND. The person who was going to PROTECT me at all costs. Well, I didn't feel protected at that moment. The moment when my mother had to plea with APD to let me leave and that I was a battered wife. My nanny was upstairs with the children, who didn't hear a thing, thank God. They released me to my mom, she let them know I had my dad's burial to attend in 2 days and I needed to go to the hospital to be checked out for a broken nose. They allowed me to leave but charged me with felony assault. I buried my dad with bruised ribs, a torn retina and knots on my head and what felt like a broken nose. But I felt free. I felt free because I knew in my heart that if I walked away at that moment, I wasn't losing anything. In fact, I was gaining, I was gaining a new life. It just took that moment to allow me to see. It was a horrific ending to my fairytale story 10 years later.

I have learned to love myself first. That's what I failed to do in any relationship. I always wanted to please someone else and make sure they were happy with ME. I don't mean everyone, but in my relationship, I wanted to please my husband and make sure he was comfortable, etc. It was frowned upon for me to take time for me and I have learned to love me first. It has been a long time for me to get to that point. It has been a daily struggle. Not a realization that came after my divorce or after Darren's murder. It has been a long time coming. You have to be strong, so you do, but you realize over time your strength is your survival. It isn't a selfish way to think. It is the only way to think. Your spiritual self-needs to be whole. As a human being, I had to learn from my mistakes in this whole struggle. I was not a flawless victim. I played a part in my own struggle. I didn't love myself because I was a "Prisoner of Love." I was a prisoner of my mind. I was holding myself back with childhood fantasies. Fantasies that I allowed to cloud my vision. Please understand I went through counseling sessions, alone and with my abusive spouse. It wasn't until later that I realized I couldn't hear or see because I had blinders on. I had tunnel vision for my life. Once I learned that after loving yourself first you allow yourself to heal and forgive. It's a process that I am at today. I have healed from this past and allowing myself to please others first. I want to be light to others, and my prayer is that I can be light to my children.

Today I am newlywed to Dejuan. We wed after 5 years of being together. We are evolving in our new lives together, growing stronger daily. We are witnessing our children become unique and confident in their journeys. I am involved with my father's estate planning. My sister and I run a foundation that we started with dad's interest in mind of giving back to children. Reaching back to people that are in need. I am at that stage in my life. I enjoy hearing people's stories of where they are from and how we connect because of similar paths. I have enjoyed my career as a doctor of pharmacy for over 20 years. Although it has been rewarding, my focus and drive today is at a different level. My passion is in what you are reading at this moment. I pray that my words have ignited, inspired, enriched, empathized and enlightened you. I pray that you find YOUR strength and survive your past. I enjoy telling my story to help someone else. It has been a process to get here and I know I still have a long way to go. I know that my life is not a tragedy. YOUR life is not a tragedy. You are here for a purpose, and that's your mission. Be the light.

Alone from night to night is where you
will find me

Too weak to break these chains that bind me
I need no shackles to remind me
I'm just a prisoner of love

She's in my dreams, awake or sleeping
Upon my knees, to her, I'm creeping
My very life is in her keeping
I'm just a prisoner of love

Don't be a PRISONER, be the light.

SURVIVOR TALK
What Is a Safety Plan?

A safety plan is a personalized, practical plan that includes ways to remain safe while in a relationship, planning to leave, or after you leave. Safety planning involves how to cope with emotions, tell friends and family about the abuse, take legal action and more.

Safety While Living With Your Abuser

- Identify your partner's use and level of force so that you can assess the risk of physical danger to you and your children before it occurs.
- Identify safe areas of the house where there are no weapons and there are ways to escape. If arguments occur, try to move to those areas.
- Don't run to where the children are, as your partner may hurt them as well.
- If violence is unavoidable, make yourself a small target. Dive into a corner and curl up into a ball with your face protected and arms around each side of your head, fingers entwined.
- If possible, have a phone accessible at all times and know what numbers to call for help. Know where the nearest public phone is located. Know the phone number to your local shelter. If your life is in danger, call the police.
- Let trusted friends and neighbors know of your situation and develop a plan and visual signal for when you need help.

- Teach your children how to get help. Instruct them not to get involved in the violence between you and your partner. Plan a code word to signal to them that they should get help or leave the house.
- Tell your children that violence is never right, even when someone they love is being violent. Tell them that neither you, nor they, are at fault or are the cause of the violence, and that when anyone is being violent, it is important to stay safe.
- Practice how to get out safely. Practice with your children.
- Plan for what you will do if your children tells your partner of your plan or if your partner otherwise finds out about your plan.
- Keep weapons like guns and knives locked away and as inaccessible as possible.
- Make a habit of backing the car into the driveway and keeping it fueled. Keep the driver's door unlocked and others locked — for a quick escape.
- Try not to wear scarves or long jewelry that could be used to strangle you.
- Create several plausible reasons for leaving the house at different times of the day or night.

Path to Safety. n.d. 30 8 2017.
<http://www.thehotline.org/help/path-to-safety/>.

Broken things can become blessed things,
if you let God do the mending.
~Wounds to Wisdom

Chapter Four

I DON'T LOOK LIKE WHAT I'VE
BEEN THROUGH
By Evangelist Detra Williams

For I know the plans I have for you," says the LORD. "They are plans for good and not for disaster, to give you a future and a hope. Jeremiah 29:11 (NLT)

I was born May 24, 1966, in Longview, Texas in a small area of town called Fox Hill. My mother was the youngest of 12 kids, and she was only 17 years old when I was born. When I was only 6 months old, my mother married the man that later became my father. I may not have his blood running through my veins, but I am every bit his twin. He moved the family to Dallas, Texas along with his mother (my grandmother). Later, there were 2 more children born from this marriage. Life as I remember started well. Parents and grandmother worked, we ate the best food, and we lived in a very nice neighborhood. But like any other family, there was a dark secret; things were not as it appeared in public because behind closed doors life was Hell. My parents were alcoholics, and my father was an abuser. He would beat my Mom with whatever he could get his hands on. But mainly he would break the broom handle and beat her with that, or he would be so mad that he would sometimes use the butt of his gun. They would always send us outside. But of course, we could hear everything, we would pretend that it did not bother us. He would not beat us as he did our mother but we sure did get some serious spankings. With all these family secrets, you would think that was all. However, at the young age of 7 years old, my life was getting worse. It was late in the midnight hour in early spring of 1974. A few months before my 8th birthday; as I slept in my bedroom that I shared with my baby sister, who was 3 years younger than me, I felt a light touch shaking my big toe. I woke up to see a dark figure standing at the end of my bed waving for me to follow him. A brief time later, I returned to my room crying and shaking, not understanding what just happened to my body.

A few months had passed, and that light touch was still shaking my big toe to wake me up. Not knowing what to do and since this had gone on for months, I decided to ask that one question, "Why are you doing this to me." The answer was very shocking. "If you were my REAL niece, I would not be doing this to you." Because he knew that the man that was raising me was not my blood father; he felt that it was ok to do these things.

In June of 1974, a few weeks after my 8th birthday, I was using the bathroom, and I wiped and noticed redness and extreme wetness on the toilet paper. I begin to scream. I really thought I was bleeding to death and I was going to die. Both my mother and grandmother had a calm reaction and in a soft voice said, "Oh she got her period, you are going to be ok." Still not understanding what was happening to my body. I guess it was normal no one got scared but me. When I had my period, I could sleep in peace knowing that the dark figure would not bother me. So, I would pray to bleed forever. But that did not happen. He would always tell me that no one would believe me and he would kill my Mommy if I told anyone. So, quietness continued for years. I'm not sure what part of the year this was but I was home alone with that dark figure, and he grabbed my hand for me to follow him into the garage. He laid me down on the floor, and the pain was worse than ever. As he continues to try to put his penis in me, it just would not go. He complained about my vagina being dry. He tried to moisten the area by using his finger, but still, there was no moisture. His head went between my legs, and I felt instant moisture as he took his saliva and spat on my vagina. After that, he could insert. This was the worse feeling in the world. He had never been so rough before, and it had never hurt so badly.

At the age of 12, I began to feel sick in the morning, and I could not hold down food. I went from an active teenager that loved playing sports to a teenager that only wanted to sleep. My mother decided to take me to the doctor. At the Doctor' office, I overheard my Mother say, who would do this to my baby? How could my 12-year-old daughter be pregnant? But she didn't ask me. However, a few days later she took me to another doctor's appointment at a different office. There was a weird smell, and people just looked at me. We went to the back, and about 30 minutes later the procedure was over. I cramped and bled so badly that all I could do was lay down. We arrived home, and a male detective was sitting in our living room. He introduced himself to me and talked to me about sports, and foods that I like. The Detective asked me who I had been having sex with. I looked him straight in his eyes and said: "a dark figure and his name is W." My mom screamed, my grandmother cried, and my father was ready to kill. He was sentenced 25 years to life (due to prior criminal history and disclosure from another child down the street). I was not prepared for the effects that this would have on the rest of my life. Before and after he had gone to prison, no one talked about what happened. No one told me that I did nothing wrong. No one even gave me a hug or said that everything was going to be alright. I began to not care about myself. I felt dirty, nasty and all I wanted to do was have sex with and anybody that wanted it. Sometimes it was 2 or 3 boys in one day. I did not care. There were no emotions attached. I felt lost and empty. At the age of 19 years old, I got married, not because of love, but because this was a way to get out of my Dad's house and on my own. I had my first child at 20 years old and divorced at the age of 22. I was right back in my Dad's house, but it was ok because he mainly lived with his girlfriend.

While trying to get my life back on track, I was working as a Receptionist at Allstate Business College. One day this young man came to my desk and gave me a Dr. Pepper; this was my favorite drink, and I had one daily. He smiled, said that I was beautiful and he wanted to do something nice for me. I thanked him, and he walked off without telling me his name. I really wasn't sure if he was a student here, but I did know that he made me smile. Smiling was something I did not do much of those days. I had the same daily routine; got off the city bus in front of the building, went to the vending machine, got my daily Dr. Pepper, walked to my desk and was ready to work. A few days had passed since that nice young man came to see me. One day I looked up and there he was; standing in front of me. My heart was beating so fast, that I felt it through my clothes. He said, "hello there beautiful, I have something for you." I told him that I already have a Dr. Pepper and he said that he had something better for me. He said that he noticed that I rode the city bus and he wanted to give me a bus pass. I was immediately taken; no one had ever done anything for me and not want something in return. He asked if he could walk me to the bus stop after work and I told him sure. I finally asked him his name, and he said L.D.; then I asked if he was a student here. He said that he was, but he was going to quit because he could not concentrate on his school work knowing that I was sitting downstairs. He said that he wanted to spend all his time with me, and boy did we spend a lot of time together. A few weeks had passed, and we became intimate with each other. Oh, My God, it was the best I ever had. His endurance lasted forever; he demanded sex every day; we would have sex in the bathroom, under the stairs, behind the building, and in empty classrooms. This man made me feel as if I was the only woman in the world. He ensured that I was always sexually satisfied. Never did I realize he was beginning to control me. Months had passed, and he was still walking me to the bus stop, bringing me flowers, candy and gave me whatever I wanted. I never asked him if he worked or how he got his money, I just knew he wanted me, and there was nothing else important. He met my son and they immediately connected. He began to bring him toys and always wanted all of us together as a family. I met his family, he met my family and we finally moved in together. Shortly after that we were married. I loved and admired everything about this man. He knew how to treat me, he loved my son, and he was willing to take me away from my dull, lonely life.

It wasn't long after we married that things began to change for the worse. One evening we were visiting his sister's house, having a really good time. It was getting late, and I had to go to work the next day. It took us a while to get home on the bus. I kept telling him that I was ready to go but he was laughing, drinking and smoking funny smelling cigarettes (later learned that it was marijuana). This was a side of him that I had never seen before; I went over and tapped him on his shoulders. What in the world did I do that for? The next thing I know he had his hands around my throat and pushed me against the wall. Everybody there just looked and was just as shocked as I was. He told me to sit my ass down, and that we would leave when he was ready to leave. I was in shock and did not know what to think. All I could do was cry and thank God, my son did not see this. The next day, I was still in shock. I was quiet and cried off and on. I had promised myself that I would never be in a relationship like my Mother and allow a man to hit me. He looked at me, said that he was sorry and that he would never do it again. He leaned over and kissed me like he had never kissed me before. I called out of work but still took my son to daycare; we spent the rest of the day in the bed having sex like never. Never did I know that sex could be this good and last so long. I had no clue this was only the beginning of my horrible ordeal.

Regardless of how many fights we had and how many times I left, coming back the sex never stopped. So, in 1990, we had our child together. I really felt that this was going to change things in our life. See, I had already had a few miscarriages because of the ongoing abuse. In September 1993, I had really had enough. He wanted me to pawn my wedding ring because he had spent his paycheck on drugs and of course he wanted more drugs. As we rode in the car, he kept telling me that we were going to pawn my ring. I stood my ground and told him a strong No! Well that did not go over well. The next thing I knew my lip was bleeding, my head was hurting, and my glasses were on the floor board of the car. Well, he won, he pawns my wedding ring, and I knew I was not going to ever see it again. On our way home he made his pit stop at the drive through drug house. (Yes the driveway was made in a "U" shape, and there was a big huge tree that sat in the middle of the driveway, that is where they sold their drugs). When we got home, his sister was at our house. She saw how I looked, and she cursed him out. It really didn't matter. She could not protect me because she was just as much of a drug addict as he was. They were in the back room, and I just could not take it anymore. The kids were gone with my mother, so I went into the bedroom and pulled out a bottle of Tylenol with codeine and took a handful of them. I cannot tell you how many; I just knew I poured them into my hand and swallowed. I looked up, and his sister was standing there. She immediately slapped me to make me spit out the pills, but it did not help. She screamed for my husband. He got mad because we interrupted his high. They called 911, and I was in the hospital for 3 days for observation and again diagnosed with chemical depression. Thank God attempted suicide failed.

Don't get me wrong there were times that I did fight back, only to make the beating worse. I remember one time, I must say that I got him good. One evening I had been talking on a cordless cell phone to my mother, well he always had the habit of when I got off the phone; he out picks it up and hit redial, to see who would answer. This time he did that and my step-father answered, my abuser immediately hung up the phone without saying anything and started in on me. He was hitting me upside the head with the cordless phone.

To protect myself as always, I covered my face then I reached over and got the fishing knife that was sitting on the dresser. See he had just gotten back from fishing earlier that day. As I grabbed the knife, while he continued to hit me, I just begin to stab him, not knowing if I was hitting him or not. But suddenly he stopped hitting me and he begins to holler that I had stabbed him. He was stabbed twice under the arm and one time 2 inches from his heart. Well yours truly went to jail; it was ok I fought back. The grand jury did not indict me because of our history of domestic violence. The cycle of leaving and coming back was still ongoing. Visit to many domestic violence shelters, protective orders and then going back was my ongoing cycle. Some would say that maybe she liked the abuse, no I didn't like it but just gave up because each time I left he would find me. He would show up at the shelter and I would get kicked out. Then I would be back with him, not sure why I kept going back I just did.

You walk around house on egg shell, not knowing if you say something that might be wrong, you will get slapped. If you don't fold the clothes the right way, cook his dinner just right or wear something that he just doesn't like. The result is that you might get slapped, pushed or kicked. There would be times that I would go to the store or window shopping with my Mom, regardless if I wanted to buy something or not; I had to buy. Mainly because I had to bring home receipts so he could see what time I checked out at one store and the time I checked out at the next store. To him if I had let too much time pass he wanted to know what I was doing and who I was with. He had always accused me of being with other men. There was this one time when I came home from work late and he had to perform what was called "an examination." He had to check my vagina to see if it was stretched out from having sex. After the examination, he wanted to brand me (mark his territory), Yes, he got a wire hanger, folded it and put it on the burner on the stove, his intent was to brand my vagina to show that I belong to him. This did not happen because the kids woke up. I could go on and on but life with an abuser is an ongoing cycle of unexplained, unpredictable moments and a lifetime of overwhelming hurtful memories.

There had been so many, from a fractured nose, bruised ribs, fractured arm, black eye, busted lips, 3 miscarriages, attempted suicide and a swollen jaw. But if I had to choose the worse one, it would be the very last time, and when I knew for sure, I was going to die. It was on a Sunday. I had gone to church, and for some reason, I had a strange feeling the whole day. All I could do was sit in church, cry and pray to God that if he got me out this time, I would stay out and never look back. See, I had left several times but only to return. Church that Sunday was great! I felt the presences of the Lord all over me, and I worshipped God like never. We went home, I cooked a great dinner, and he and the boys were playing. We were a very happy family. It begins to get late. He had bathed the boys and put them to bed. He was an excellent father to the boys. He did everything for them. I was in the kitchen cleaning up and singing, "Because he lives" (which was my favorite hymn). He came into the kitchen, got some water and asked me to sit down. I was still smiling and just loving life; he looked at me and said that God told him to kill me today. I did not respond. I just looked because I was shocked at what he just said. He looked me straight in my eyes and said, "You are going to die tonight." Then he slapped me so hard, he busted my lip, and it was gushing blood. As I was sitting there holding a hand full of blood, he kept looking at the picture of God that we had hanging on the wall, he kneeled and said, "God, I hear you." I was still sitting in the chair, holding the blood in my hands. He told me to go into the bathroom, and he followed me. He got a towel with cold water and was cleaning the blood off my face and held the towel on my lip. We went into the bedroom; he closed the door and told me to get out of my clothes. I stripped down to only my socks. Then it begins! He slapped me, hit me in the stomach, and hit me again and again all over my body. But what was so amazing was that I could not cry or scream, and this made him mad; He tried to grab the iron that was sitting on the edge of the dresser, but he could not get it because it was plugged in behind the dresser. So, he grabbed a can of clothing starch and began to hit me in the head. He had hit me so hard that I really thought I was going to pass out, but I never did. Again, I could not scream nor could I cry; this escalated him even more. He kept saying "bitch you gonna die."

I stood there with only my socks on, holding my face between my hands as he continued to hit me with the can of starch. Then he said, you think I am playing with you. He opened the bedroom door and headed to the kitchen. I stood there in the doorway just starring at the front door that was chained and locked. I could hear him in the kitchen going through the utensil drawer. I said to myself "he is looking for the knife." He hadn't realized that I had washed dishes and the knife was under other dishes that were drying. During the whole ordeal, I did not cry, scream, nor was I praying. It felt like I was standing in the bedroom doorway forever.

Everything was in slow motion. I began to pray for God to take care of my children, and not let them hurt or be hurt. Lord, take care of my family, and don't let them hurt because I am dead; but God if it be your will, I will live and not die. I began to sing in my head "Because he lives." Again, everything was moving in slow motion, and I could still hear him looking for the knife. Within seconds of me praying and singing, I had opened my eyes and looked down the hall, and the front door swung open. I did not think twice. I ran as if my life depended on it and to be honest it did. I ran through the apartment complex still only wearing my socks, until I saw a light on in this apartment. I knocked on the door and was screaming help!!

During the entire time, he was beating on me I did not say a word. But that time I cried out for help; the man opened the door and took one look at me and said get in here. Now, remember I was naked but it did not faze him at all; All he saw was a woman that was bleeding from various parts of her face and body. He immediately got me some sweatpants and t-shirt to put on. He did not ask any questions, and he called 911. The police arrived. The pushed this nice man against the wall and were beginning to handcuff him, and I say "No! It was not him, he was only helping me." I explained what had happened and by the time the police got to the apartment, he was gone, and the kids were still in their beds. They were fine but had been crying. Two days later I appeared in court for my protective order. The judge looked at the pictures that were taken by the police, and then asked to see my identification. I asked him why? He said look at these pictures and look at you now. You are not the same person. To be honest, I wasn't the same person in more ways than one. The night of the incident my face was so swollen that it was two times its size, my head was swollen for being beat with the can of starch. The judge asked me what I did. I told him that I did not do anything that it was all God. He looked at me and said, I told the truth. Now my new life slowing begins.

The most important lesson that I learned was if he hits you once, he will hit you again. I don't care how much they say I'm sorry, or I will never do it again. I don't care how good the sex is, when the honeymoon is over, well it's over, and the abuse will begin again. This cycle never ends. It will be your life or theirs, but most of the time it will be yours. There are several counseling and therapy that could assist the abuser, but as with anything the abuser must want to change and the help.

Wow! I never thought life would be the way it is now. I have accomplished so much all because of the Favor and the Grace of God. In July of 1997, I moved to Fayetteville, NC because I met a man over the phone. Yes, it sounds strange, but I do feel that this was God's plan. I moved here, got a job and began to live a normal life, or at least what I thought was normal. It wasn't easy because I still feared that this man would one day hit me and I might not escape this time. What made this different was that he knew what I had been through. I did not want to hide what I had experienced in my previous relationship, plus it explained some of my weird behavior.

Over time, things got better; the kids had moved here from Texas, and they were enjoying life, school, and sports. We were finally happy, and living like a family should be living. We married in 1999; God blessed me with 2 stepchildren and later 2 wonderful grandchildren. I was blessed with some very outstanding jobs with only a high school diploma. Although I wanted more, I was afraid because I never thought of myself as being successful. But then God surrounded me with people who believed in me, more than I believed in myself, and they saw something in me. I began going to college in October 2007, became an Ordained Minister in September 2009, and graduated college with a bachelor degree in Social Work in December 2012. I then got a job in County Government working in Child Protective Services as a Forensic Social Worker. Primarily working with sexually abused children. Now, I really did not know how I was going to handle this, but thanks be to God, he gave me the strength to do just what he had equipped me to do. While working with these children, I was still working on myself; I still had low self-esteem and feared what people thought of me. I always had a smile on my face, and no one ever knew my story. I became a member of a support group named Survivors & Conqueror. They focus on women who have been sexually, physically, emotionally abused, raped, divorced and used the tools that God has already equipped us with to be healed and delivered from being physically and sexually abused through the Word of God. When I say that this group changed my life! The healing part was easy, the forgiveness took time, but the deliverance took a while. God did just what he said he was going to do when I activated my faith in Him. My faith in God helped me to conqueror that Mountain and I was completely delivered from the things of the past. Now, it took a village of true prayer warriors, true believers, and an awesome support system to get me to this point. The journey was not easy and I could not have done it alone. I am now able to devote my attention to the children he has placed in my life.

I have mentored woman who have been and are currently in an abusive relationship without passing judgment on them. I have been able to tell my story to many and have been a shoulder for them to lean on. March of 2017, I graduated with my Master's Degree in Human Services, and I know this is not the end. My assignment in this life is not complete; I am preparing myself mentally for what God will lead me to do.

I know it is not easy to see the bright light at the end of the tunnel when you are in an abusive relationship but there is a bright light, and it is there to lead you out of Hell. People will never understand domestic violence unless they have gone through it themselves. All the negative comments, the eyes rolling and backs being turned. I often still hear people say, that they would not let a man hit them. Well, I said the same thing repeatedly. But as I look back over my life realizing that the abuse started at such an early age. I never received counseling or therapy never being told that I did not do anything wrong. So, I grew up thinking that everything I got in life I deserved it.

You must want more for yourself, and you must be willing to put in the work to be a better person. Unfortunately, due to the multiple beating, the consist blows/hits to my head; this has affected my long-term memory. When my boys would ask me if I remember certain things from their childhood, I hate to say it but I don't. My youngest son in now a father and he ask questions such as, what age did I crawl, walk and start talking and I don't remember. The physical effects of domestic violence are gone, except for the ridge of my nose you can feel the knot where it was fractured, and inside my bottom lip there is still the scar of where my lip had been busted several times. The emotional effects of domestic violence take a lifelong process of healing.

I often say, if I had to do it all over, again would I? Sounds like a hard question to answer but it's not. I don't think I would have changed anything I had gone through. Although it was not pleasant and I almost lost my life many times. I do believe I would not be the person I am today if I had a different past. There is so much more to tell, but most importantly, I am a survivor of domestic violence, and I don't look like what I have been through.

I Don't Look Like What I've Been Through

I have had years of heartache; I have had years of pain. I have even had years of disgrace and many years of shame. I have even been persecuted and misused, But I don't look like what I been through.
The devil tried to steal all my dreams and then he tried to take all my joy too. He put hopelessness in cruise control so I'd lose control and take my own life. See, I don't look like what I've been through.
That small voice of suicide entered my head yes, it came. I was molested and my innocence taken from me. Asked what were you wearing? What did you do? NO HUGS, NO LOVE, only humiliation, and shame. But I don't look like what I've been through.
Told I was fat, ugly, nobody wants you but me. Black-eyes,

fractured nose, busted lip, bruised ribs, all in the name of love. Beaten, raped, sodomized and I had to shed so many tears; feared it was about to get worse. That voice of suicide entered my head, pills went down my throat. Stomach pumped, diagnosed with post-traumatic stress syndrome and depression. But I don't look like what I've been through.

Today, I don't look like I was molested, I don't look like I was beaten, I don't look like rape, and I don't even look like suicide. But what I do look like is God's Grace; I look like God's Mercy, I look like the Sun shining after the storm.

Tears of joy in my eyes.

God, you opened the windows of Heaven, the wind blew in Grace then Mercy followed, and that is why I can shout without a doubt that I am more than a Survivor! I am more than a conqueror! I can say I AM HEALED, DELIVERED AND HAVE BEEN SET FREE! I'm just telling you my story, don't know what you would do…Just want to let you know that I don't look like what I've been through.

SURVIVOR TALK
Feeling Free

Freedom: The quality or state of being free: as

The absence of necessity, coercion, or constraint in choice or action. Liberation from slavery or restraint or from the power of another: Independence. The quality or state of being exempt or released usually from something onerous. The quality of being frank, open or outspoken. Boldness

- What makes you feel free?
- What makes you feel controlled?
- Do you have a feeling of rebellion when you feel that you want to be free?

From every wound there is a scar, and every scar tells a story.
A story that is your testimony.
~Wounds to Wisdom

Chapter Five

UNWANTED INHERITANCE
By Lakesia Muhammad

"But the meek will inherit the land and enjoy
peace and prosperity"
Psalm 37:11

I grew up in a single parent home with my younger sister. My mother was a strong & independent woman, who worked hard but had many failed relationships. The man who came around sporadically was my sister's father. I thought very highly of him; however, after discovering that he was a married man explained why his visits were so sporadic.

Most of my early years were spent at the home of my paternal grandparents. My grandparents played an instrumental role in my upbringing, and I often went to church with my grandmother, ultimately giving me that spiritual foundation that I carry to this day. I was also able to spend time with my father who resided with them. Although he was physically present, I never got that moral and spiritual guidance that could have possibly helped me in choosing a mate. My father was young, carefree, and very much a ladies' man. However, I do know that my father loved me, but not able to provide the support that I needed because of the poor choices he made in his life.

My early years were equally spent with my maternal family, but a great deal of dysfunction was present. I can remember a lot of alcohol consumption and witnessing terrible "throw down" fights between my mother & her siblings. This was very scary & disturbing to me as a child. As an adult, family secrets were revealed to me and would explain some of the fights I had witnessed. In those days, a child was seen and not heard, but in the quiet of my thoughts, I knew this was not behavior I wanted to adopt as an adult. Through the dysfunction, there was still that sense of a "family stick together" no matter what. This duality was very conflicting in my mind.

Fast forward to the summer of 1988, I was 16 years old and introduced to who would later become my husband, father of my children and abuser.

He was a star high school football player, and so fine. That summer was so magical, and I can still remember the rap song "I ain't no Joke" by Eric B & Rakim as he loudly blasted, while "flossing" in his uncle's truck. I knew this was not his truck, but I was so smitten with love and adoration, it didn't matter, all I knew is that he was coming to visit me and sport me around like a trophy. Young attractive teenagers with no inhibitions, we fell in love very quickly. That entire summer he was my world, and I experienced many of my 'firsts" with him. My "first "time getting drunk, (40 oz Old English was his choice of drink) "first" time smoking weed, and my "first" REAL sexual experience. Although "firsts" for me, they were not for him. Drinking was something he had been doing since age 13 or 14.

Our growing relationship caused problems between me and my mother at home. I began showing signs of rebellion by skipping school, lying, and staying out past my curfew to be with him. My mother always saw him as disrespectful and didn't like him much. In our hometown, it seemed like everybody knew everybody and my mother knew his father who owned a tavern at that time. She knew of him to be an abuser and womanizer, and in her mind the "Apple don't fall too far from the tree." Against my mother's advice, we remained a couple throughout high school. He was a year ahead of me, so he graduated first, and went off to college in another state. I was devastated and made many visits to see him.

While he was away at school, I developed a relationship with his mother and began, learning about his family history. I learned that he had anger and behavioral issues as a young boy in school and it was documented. I also learned that his father was a GREAT deal older than she was, and became pregnant at a very young age. She also shared with me, that his father was not only a married man but displayed acts of violence toward her. This raised an eyebrow for me but never thought this may be a generational cycle.

It is now 1990, and we have our first child together. One of those many visits to see him in school resulted in my becoming pregnant. Two years later, we decided to get married and give our child what we didn't have, a stable family. However, the abuse had begun with him jumping in my face during arguments to intimidate, grabbing, pushing & shoving me. By this time, he was also staying out late, drinking and cheating. As a matter of fact, he later told me that the night before we got married; he had been out all night with another woman. By 1997, we had 3 children, and the abuse continued both verbally and physically. We argued about everything from religion to what our children's name would be, his drinking as well as his continued infidelity.

You're probably wondering why I stayed this long; well I loved him, wanted to keep my family together, and thought that maybe God wanted me to hang in there because my understanding was, God hates divorce.

By 2001, the babies kept coming and now on child number four. A few years later we briefly moved to Maryland, where he taught school. Hard to imagine that someone responsible for helping to mold & shape future minds could behave so poorly, (that's another discussion) Anyways while living in Maryland, I was very miserable, never got a job, I had no family or friends and felt very isolated. At the time our children were 12, 7, 5 & 2, and were all in school except for my 2-year-old.

One morning before he went to work, we had a heated argument. This was an argument we'd been having for the past 5 years regarding one of my son's names being changed. He wanted his name to be after his, but I had refused to change the name. My son was often referred to as "the boy" and caused major tension in the house because everyone was afraid to call him by the name that I had given him.

On this morning, he got so angry that he jumped on top of me and restrained my arms with one hand while covering my mouth with the other. As my 5-year-old son lay sleeping within inches of me, he began to violate me. I used the term violate, but it was RAPE!!

Paralyzed with fear, I could not believe that this was happening. He got up, showered, and went off to work like nothing happened. This was it! I had to get the hell out of here, but I was hundreds of miles away from home and no money, how am I going to get out I thought.

I called home to tell my mother what happened and of

course, she was very concerned. However, I assured her that I would get home along with my children. I made contact with a friend who wired money to me, and a neighbor who I'd like to refer to as "The Angel Next Door" arranged for me and my four children to get to the bus station in Washington DC.

As I quickly began packing our things, I heard him pull up, "Oh My God he's going to see me packing" I thought. He entered the house stood there with this look of rage, but said nothing, grabbed something and left. With a sigh of relief, I continued packing. That day my oldest daughter was the only one in school, so I had to arrange to get her and gather the others so that we could get out of there before he got home. Time was ticking, and I had to act fast. I managed to grab as much as I could, gather the children, and off we were to the bus station. During the ride to the bus station, I recall feeling like a runaway slave, trying to gain my freedom, and my "Angel Next Door" became my Harriet Tubman.

After discovering that the children and I had left, I was warned by another neighbor, that they saw him pack up the car, and may be possibly headed back to our hometown. Well, they were correct, he appeared the next day after we had gotten there. During the first couple of weeks of returning home, the children and I stayed with my mother, and I had been very sick. I was experiencing nausea and vomiting just before leaving Maryland but attributed it to stress. Needless to say, this was a very familiar sickness I had experienced four times before; YES, I was pregnant for the fifth time. NO GOD, not again! I quietly screamed out while sitting in the doctor's office, I cannot bring another child into this situation. Well, God makes no mistake; I had a miscarriage that same week that I received the news. However, we ended up reconciling shortly after; Crazy, Right? But I had a plan, so I thought.

I walked on egg shells for the next few months, and this man even had the audacity to imply the possibility of me aborting the child I miscarried, but I shook it off and had to make him think that I was trying to work it out. Once again, the topic of changing my son's name emerged, and I thought he would let it go if I calmly explained to him why I didn't want to do it. Wrong! Another heated argument about this issue led to him grabbing me and forcing me to sign papers for a name change that he had drawn up by a lawyer. I signed them because I was afraid and found myself back in the same situation that I got away from while in Maryland. This time I knew I had to quickly think of a way to get out.

I went to Family Court and got an Order of Protection without him knowing. I chose one of the coldest days to finally do what I should have done a long time ago. As he prepared to run errands, I quietly took his key ring and slid off the house key. I anxiously waited for him to leave, as he acted like he was such a loving husband asking me what I needed while he was out. Please!! Just leave I thought. He finally left; I watched him pull off and REJOICED! Conflicted in my feelings, I began thinking about what am I going to tell my children, but I couldn't turn back.

A few hours later he returned, and I stood by the door as I heard him fumble with the keys trying to figure out why none of them would work. I could hear him mumbling something, and he began ringing the doorbell like a maniac. I yelled through the door that it was over, I have an order of protection and that I had called the police. As you can probably imagine, he was enraged by this time, and yelling and screaming outside the door. The police showed up, he got his clothes while saying nasty things to me and to sum it up, that was the end of the marriage but not the end of the abuse.

Thirteen years later, happily remarried to a loving & devoted husband, with whom I share a son. My ex-husband continues to abuse emotionally, & verbally, through our four children. They have been deeply affected by the back and forth to family court for custody, child support, etc. I'd have to say that my oldest child has been the most affected. Now an adult, my oldest child has experienced violence and abuse in her young life. I believe that girls tend to choose mates who are like or similar to their father. She displayed rebellion as a teenager by running away from home, drinking, and hanging out with the wrong crowd. In 2012 the unthinkable happened when she was a victim of gun violence being in the wrong place at the wrong time. Thankfully she survived. Through it all, my children remain resilient and continue overcoming all obstacles against the odds. My oldest still struggles with her past experiences but is taking it one day at a time, my second oldest is a college graduate, while the others are finishing high school and college. My continued prayer is that this vicious cycle ends here.

As you can see, inheritance is not just about money or property. It can be a cycle of dysfunction, abuse, and violence that has a trickledown effect. So, I appeal to you, heed the early warning signs, pay attention to certain behaviors, and most importantly ask God to order your steps in choosing a mate so that you are not a recipient of an "Unwanted Inheritance."

SURVIVOR TALK
Journaling

Writing in a journal is an effective tool for use in the healing process. It can help to process not only failed relationships but also to recover from grief and loss.

If you want to improve your perspective on life and clarify issues, start writing in a journal. You can't know where you're going if you don't know where you are.

Here are 10 tips to get started:

1. Start writing about where you are in your life at this moment. Describe your living situation, your work, and your relationships. Are you right where you want to be?

2. For five to ten minutes just start writing in a "stream of consciousness." Don't edit your thoughts or feelings and don't correct your grammar. Don't censor your thoughts.

3. Start a dialogue with your inner child by writing in your subdominant hand. Answer with your dominant hand. What issues emerge?

4. Cultivate an attitude of gratitude by maintaining a daily list of things you appreciate, including uplifting quotes. Keep it in one journal or in a separate section so that you can read through it all at once. When you feel down you can read through it for a boost of gratitude and happiness.

5. Start a journal of self-portraits. You can take pictures, draw colors or shapes or collage images. Learn to love and accept yourself just the way you are today.

6. Keep a nature diary to connect with the natural world. The world we live in is a magical and mysterious place. Record the things you notice about the sky, the weather, and the seasons.

7. Maintain a log of successes. Begin by writing the big ones you remember then regularly jot down small successes that occur during the week. As you pay attention, your list will grow and inspire you.

8. Keep a log or playlist of your favorite songs. Write about the moods they evoke. When you hear a song that triggers a strong memory, write down how you feel and explore that time and space of your life.

9. If there's something you are struggling with or an event that's disturbing you, write about it in the third person. This will give you distance and provide a new perspective. Write down what you learned about yourself.

10. Develop your intuition. Write down questions or concerns then take a deep breath and listen for a response from your Higher Self. Let yourself write automatically. If you don't get an answer right away, look for signs during the day.

We all have dark days, black moods, and anxious feelings. Use writing in a journal to explore the darkness. You will find your inner light when you do.

Hills, C. Loran. *10 Journaling Tips to Help You Heal, Grow and Thrive.* n.d. 7 September 2017. <https://tinybuddha.com/blog/10-journaling-tips-to-help-you-heal-grow-and-thrive/>.

God is not punishing you, He's preparing you.
~Wounds to Wisdom

Chapter Six

THROUGH A SON'S LENS
By Roderick Cunningham

There was never a great man who had not a great mother.
~Olive Schreiner

Born in Talladega Alabama Roderick and his brothers grew up around wide open fields, a restaurant, hard-working great-grandparents, grandparents, uncles, and aunts. Their mother Beverly was a short 5-foot 4inch woman full of love, kindness, and positive energy. Beverly grew up to humble beginnings in Talladega as well. However, that loving women suffered much even in her childhood. Her mother was married to a verbally, physically, and financially abusive husband. At a young age, it would be decided that Beverly, and her older sister and younger brother would live with their grandparent's due to the emotion and physical abuse in the home. The abuse that Beverly, and her siblings endured during their child should never happen to any child. 1 and 4 women nationally will experience some form of abuse in their lifetime. Some women are choked; some a gun to the head; others beat; others are told they are worthless and will never be anything. How then should a soul respond? Abuse seems to be a norm in the emotion and physical abuse in the home. The abuse that Beverly, and her siblings endured during their child should never happen to any child. 1 and 4 women nationally will experience some form of abuse in their lifetime. Some women are choked; some a gun to the head; others beat; others are told they are worthless and will never be anything. How then should a soul respond? Abuse seems to be a norm in the Christian homes. Even some pastor, deacons, and the elders of churches are abusers. Abuse always seems to get covered up in most churches. How does a person heal from these many forms of abuse if even the officials in the churches are acting in the same manners of abuse to their own wives? According to Fatality Reviews done by multiple states, Domestic Violence is the leading cause of injury to women. More than car accidents, muggings, and rapes combined. And studies suggest that up to 10 million children witness some form of domestic violence annually. Every day in the U. S. more than three women are murdered by their husband, domestic partner, or boyfriend. Every 9 seconds in the U. S. a woman is assaulted or beaten.

Beverly's father never really acknowledged and spent time with her as a child. But on the other hand, Beverly's grandfather, grandmother, Uncle Billy, Aunt Jessie, his children, and their family would come and get her from her grandparents' house and spend that quality time with her. So at least she knew that side of her family. Still, the fact remains, the hurt remains that Beverly's father did not fully acknowledge her as his daughter publicly or privately. This hurt Beverly emotion from a child, into her teen years, and into her adult life. You see Beverly would watch other children spending time with their father and mother but, Beverly always had a missing piece. Her elder son Roderick would have the same issue of longing for his father until he was 35years of age. Beverly and her older sibling next to her would have three different fathers. Carolyn, Beverly, and

Ronnie were very close. They share laughs together, partied together, cried together, and comforted each other. They all had their own pain. Growing up under these conditions can leave a great negative impact on a child's life that can affect their lives forever unless the right soul connects, counsels, and brings healing to their life. Common symptoms of children under five are sleeping disruptions, withdrawal or lack of responsiveness, developmental regression or loss of acquired skills, intense anxiety, worries, increased aggression or impulsive behavior. Children 7 to 11 experience nightmares, aggression and difficulties with peers in school, emotional numbing, and school avoidance. Children ages 13 to 18 experience antisocial behavior, school failure, substance abuse, running away, violent or abusive dating relationships, depression, and withdrawal. If your children are experiencing these types of signs, seek help. Studies from The National Survey of Children's Exposure to Violence has shown that one in fifteen children exposed to intimate partner violence between parents or between parents and partners will become abusers or be willing to take abuse. This is the unfortunate effect of trauma on children exposed to domestic violence.

Beverly became pregnant with Roderick her senior year in high school. She ended up being a single mom struggling without his father. She worked at Talladega County Schools in the cafeteria. And with the help of her grandparent Beverly was able to take care of Roderick. So many mothers go through similar situations. But, through prayer and families support mothers make it through.

Then Beverly got married in the late 70's. She was so happy! She finally had a ring on it! He had a nice job! A place she could call her own. Beverly had obtained a certain level of peace of mind. You talk about happy. To this union brought two more children Quincy and Demetrius. All was good on the farm. Yes, I said farm. You see his parent had and still have acres of land. Actually, that's how her son Roderick learned how to drive. On the farm driving the tractors and washing the cars Saturday for Sunday morning church. All Beverly could think of was her children and the fact that she did not want to go through what her mother went through. Beverly and her husband would go on dates, go to church services, or whatever they had to do, and Beverly's younger sisters would watch Roderick, Quincy. Then several years later the arguing started. The arguing continued for several years. There could be many reasons for their many separations, and eventually divorce. But, verbal abuse was definitely one of the deciding factors. You see one partner's unwanted control over another in an intimate partner relationship is called Domestic Violence. Now biblically men have certain rights, and women have certain rights over each other as it relates to the levels of responsibilities of life. A nation can rise no higher than its women and when we as men learn to lift our women up we then will be lifted up as well.

In 1981 her youngest son Demetrius was born. Demetrius had holes in his heart and was sick in the hospital in Birmingham, Alabama for a while. Roderick was hurt that his new brother was sick and there was nothing he could do. Beverly and Roderick's stepfather spent a lot of time at the hospital, especially during the first years. Then the doctors told Roderick's mother and stepfather that Demetrius would be hearing impaired for the rest of his life. This was heart breaking for both parents. They often wondered why. Demetrius went through surgery to make the necessary repairs. So even though Beverly and her husband separated and eventually got a divorce. Beverly ended up being the primary caregiver for her son Demetrius. Quincy decided to stay with his father, and Demetrius and I were with our mother.

So, in the late 80's Beverly moved back in with her grandparents. Roderick can remember his mother getting calls from her husband with him trying to get back together. The conversation would always end in an argument and a slamming of the phone.

In the late 90's Beverly met this smooth talking older dude who owned a restaurant in the City of Talladega. Ada's House of Ribs. Named after his mother. Man, this was some of the best BBQ. The restaurant was successful. He was making plenty of money. Then this smooth-talking Chicago dude asked Beverly to come work for him. You know! To watch his money. He felt the other girls and staff was stealing from him. You see the restaurant was right next to Talladega College right in the midst of downtown. Through conversation, Beverly explains her life to this smooth-talking Chicago dude. She explained that she is tired of being hurt, misused, and abused. "Baby I would never do such a thing," he said. So Beverly was hesitant and would not date him. But she keeps working. Beverly has money coming in, no mortgage to pay, her children are good, she has some form of happiness at this point. The first husband was still in the life of his sons.

One day Beverly decides to date the smooth-talking Chicago dude. Oh, he was wining and dining her! And she seemed happy. But, she knew if she got serious. There was a package deal. "Her and the children." Even though he was saying out of his mouth, it did not matter. How would it really be? Some time passed, and they were dating. Beverly eventually married the smooth-talking Chicago dude. Sometime later he decided he wanted to try his luck in Georgia. Ada's House of Ribs was not pulling in what it needed financially. So the move happened. Then he was from job to Job, landing Beverly homeless for a while and having to live in a shelter. Then he became controlling and abusive physically, emotionally. Beverly had jobs but could not work like she wanted at this point in her life because her son needed care and she did not trust everyone with her son. So, Beverly being a strong black woman started an in-home childcare right in her apartment. Beverly got licensed, and she was doing well. That smooth-talking Chicago dude was always between jobs. So, Beverly held the apartment down and made sure the bills got paid. Eventually, Roderick would come to stay with his mother and stepfather. Beverly's husband was nice at first to Roderick but eventually became abusive by whipping him for the smallest of things. Beverly would jump in to defend her son. All Beverly could think of is another abuse home. Where's the love, comfort, and compassion of a loving husband? "Someone not like her own stepfather." Many families need counseling, someone to talking to, someone to relieve the anger, someone to ease the childhood memories. Women specifically, and men this is not your fault. Seek help. Don't be embarrassed. Many persons are going through similar issues. Getting help is a form of breaking the generational curses. Talk to your real friends, pastoral care, or a counselor. Those friends that stand with you and you stand with them at all times. Those friends that you can call at 3am and they will be at your door step to comfort you.

Then there was the third marriage with Leroy. "The same name of her stepfather." This guy was a talker. He wanted to be seen. The star of whatever was going on. Now he did work hard and promised to take Beverly out of the apartment and put her into a house. So, they dated. Now, this was something different because he was not the church going guy. He was the old school club guy with the silk shirts, wide bottom slacks, and gators. Needless to say, Beverly was still seeking to be loved just like any other women. And he accepted her son Demetrius, Quincy, and Roderick. To this day I don't know what Beverly really saw in him. It must have been potential. Now he did treat her like a queen for at least the first seven years. And he did put her in the house as promised and added onto the house for her daycare. Beverly was very involved with the COGIC in Decatur, Georgia. She served on the usher board, in the choir, and in pastoral care. Eventually, Beverly became an Evangelist with the COGIC. Beverly had always loved ministry. His thing was the club scene and playing cards, dominos, and drinking. But, I think she thought she could change him. Beverly did convince him to go back home and re-engage with his family. Wow! He actually listened and had a great time. Roderick can even remember his father and family coming to the wedding. The family outings in the backyard were always good. Quincy would help his mother prepare. And Quincy would always BBQ. Roderick was in Atlanta for processing with the U.S. Secret Service. He was in Atlanta while his wife and daughter were back in New Jersey.

Eventually, when he got laid off from his job, things started to change. He began to be verbally abusive. The drinking increased. And he wanted to be in total control. Beverly wanted a divorce. Some days would be good and some days would be emotional hurtful for Beverly. According to audio tapes that were made, he deeply Beverly verbally during arguments. After years, Leroy decided that he wanted to take matters into his own hand. He decided to go to the club, then he came home after midnight, woke Beverly up and started an argument. He got his gun and on October 27, 2009, Leroy shot Beverly point blank in the head. According to the DeKalb County Police, Beverly was instantly killed.

Roderick and Demetrius were nearby in the other room. And Roderick heard his mother's last words "What Are You Going To Do With That Gun" Poow..... Roderick banged on their bedroom door..."Momma" are you ok... With No Answer... Leroy came to the door "Your MF Momma Dead." Leroy walked away from Roderick. Roderick then called the DeKalb County Police 911. Roderick got Demetrius out of the house. Roderick can remember hearing the scream of his wife "Muqueet." Roderick's wife was very close to her Mother in Law Beverly. Roderick was frozen in the moment. And Roderick was trying to hold it together. Roderick and his brother were taken to the police station. Roderick made an official report. Roderick's aunts and uncles came from Alabama. Bonnie drove Roderick back to his mother's house. The family was there upon arrival. Emotions were high, and Roderick broke down. This is a day that Roderick will never forget. WSBTV Channel 2 came to Beverly's home to interview the family.

Roderick carries his mother memory through The

Beverly Cunningham Outreach Program, Inc. And his brother Quincy carries his mother's memory through "Bell's BBQ & More" in Talladega, Alabama. Roderick is grateful for his great grandparents Willie and Viola Cunningham for filling the void of a father for his mother, aunt, uncle, and stepping in as a father for Roderick. On a personal note Roderick's great grandfather taught him about GOD, Life, and how to work hard.

What does the healing process look like for me?
1. Willingness to pray, reconcile, and find it in my heart to forgive.
2. Allow myself to move to the next phase of your life. This takes a sense of personal faith, and encouraging yourself.
3. Now step out on that faith, and move forward with your life.
4. Find your sense of purpose. It will be fulfilling.
5. Find a mentor.
6. Now that you have found your purpose. Plan.
7. Now share yourself with the world to bless it with the creator's gifts.

And then Roderick's meeting face to face with Leroy in prison. To be continued......

If you are going through a domestic violence circumstance, please get help. Here's the national domestic violence hotline number. National Domestic Violence Hotline: 1.800.799.7233. Every 9 seconds in the U.S. a woman is assaulted or beaten... 19% of domestic violence involves weapons. Only 34% of people who are injured by intimate partners receive medical care for their injuries. The Economic Effect. Victims of domestic violence lose a total of 8milion days of paid work a year. Please talk to your Human Resources or Loss Prevention Personnel as a resource. The cost of domestic violence exceeds 8.3 billion annually...

Every person deserves a normalcy of life. Find Your Peace, Joy, And Happiness Again. You deserve it!!!

SURVIVOR TALK
How to help an abused friend or family member

ACKNOWLEDGE THAT THEY ARE IN A VERY DIFFICULT AND SCARY SITUATION, BE SUPPORTIVE AND LISTEN. Let them know that the abuse is not their fault. Reassure them that they are not alone and that there is help and support out there. It may be difficult for them to talk about the abuse. Let them know that you are available to help whenever they may need it. What they need most is someone who will believe and listen.

BE NON-JUDGMENTAL. Respect your friend or family member's decisions. There are many reasons why victims stay in abusive relationships. They may leave and return to the relationship many times. Do not criticize their decisions or try to guilt them. They will need your support even more during those times.

IF THEY END THE RELATIONSHIP, CONTINUE TO BE SUPPORTIVE OF THEM. Even though the relationship was abusive, your friend or family member may still feel sad and lonely once it is over. They will need time to mourn the loss of the relationship and will especially need your support at that time.

ENCOURAGE THEM TO PARTICIPATE IN ACTIVITIES OUTSIDE OF THE RELATIONSHIP WITH FRIENDS AND FAMILY. Support is critical and the more they feel supported by people who care for them, the easier it will be for them to take the steps necessary to get and stay safe away from their abusive partner.

ENCOURAGE THEM TO TALK TO PEOPLE WHO CAN PROVIDE HELP AND GUIDANCE. Find a local domestic violence agency that provides counselling or support groups. Call 1-800-799-SAFE (7233) to get a referral to one of these programs near you. Offer to go with them. If they have to go to the police, court or lawyer's office, offer to go along for moral support.

REMEMBER THAT YOU CANNOT "RESCUE" THEM. Although it is difficult to see someone you care about get hurt, ultimately, they are the one who has to make the decisions about what they want to do. It's important for you to support them no matter what they decide, and help them find a way to safety and peace.

Help a Friend or Family Member . n.d. 7 September 2017. <http://www.thehotline.org/help/help-for-friends-and-family/>.

Chapter Seven

I BROKE THE CYCLE
From Childhood Domestic Violence Victim
To Overcomer And Advocate!
By Kimberly Claborn

*And we know that in all things God works for the good of
those who love Him, who are called according to
his purpose for them.*
Romans 8:28:

The cycle of domestic violence between my parents
started early on into their relationship and became more
intense at my birth. My mother met my father when she was
18. She was still in High School and was about to graduate.
She had taken off with him around her High School
graduation, and my family had to track her down for her to
even attend her graduation ceremony. He had already had
that hold on her early on. I was born soon after. When he
found out she was pregnant with me, he dumped her out in
her parent's yard and had nothing more to do with her. Once
she gave birth to me, he came back around and slowly began
gaining more control of her. He would make her leave me
with his alcoholic mother, who would black out drunk and I
would be a newborn baby left alone in an apartment. My
mother would climb out a window to see her family. Early
into my birth, my grandparents noticed the signs of control
and neglect. He would not allow my mother to get me
healthcare. I was always crying and was underweight. The

government assistance my parents had, my father took control of that as well. It got so severe my grandparents decided to take my mother, their own daughter, to court to get custody of me because of my father's behavior. I am now 27 and have read all my court documents, and it states he would come into my grandparents' home to try and get me, shove my grandmother into a wall and was very violent. All through the custody battle, my grandparents were granted emergency custody of me and my father was told if he would take anger management and follow what the judge had set out for him, they could possibly get me back. He refused. He has a family history of alcoholism, and he has picked up that trait. My grandparents were granted full legal custody of me from then on. During my childhood, my grandparents were ordered to take me to visit my mother once a week. My mother has never had a vehicle or a driver's license. We would go to dinner, shopping, arcades. I never had to see my father.

December 1997 was when my little sisters were born, two beautiful twin girls! And that's when the control got even more intense. I was only 7 at the time, so I wasn't aware that this wasn't normal. When they were born, we could only come and visit when my father said it was okay, and when we did, we were not allowed to leave their apartment. He would leave the house but made sure my mom understood under no circumstances were we allowed to leave their house together. If we wanted to go somewhere, we would have to put my sisters in their strollers and walk down the road. I never knew what a holiday or birthday was like with my mom and sisters. He started to isolate them from the family from an early age. I remember when we would go visit my sisters, they would cry and beg us not to leave, and beg to come over. We didn't know how to explain to them that their father would not allow them to. Seeing them started to become less frequent, and when we did we were not allowed to go out in public together, those were my father's "rules." He then lost his job, and that's when the financial abuse aspect of it all set in. They never had much throughout their childhood, but we never knew how severe it was until my sister was about 14 when she called me one day and had a friend's mom get on the phone. The lady proceeded to tell me my sister had been living with them for 6 months, my parents never call and ask if she needs anything or if she would like to come home. She and her husband had decided to take in my sister due to allegations of abuse and neglect. They were going to fight for custody. My sister then started to reveal all that was happening at home. Our dad was not working, would sit at home all day and drink. He would take my mother's entire paycheck for himself, use it to buy huge amounts of alcohol and cigarettes and whatever else he wanted, which left them without food and basic necessities.

That's when I knew I was going to have to make the ultimate decision to do what was best for my sisters. Now that I was an adult myself, I had to do the right thing to make sure they were safe. That year was 2011, and that was the first time I ever I got to spend the holidays with at least one of my sisters and the first time I ever got to be out in public alone with her. I took her, and her friends to Six Flags and we had the best time! I called my mother, explained to her I would really like to talk to her about something important. My father never liked her talking on the phone, and would make her hang up in a matter of minutes. I finally had the chance to talk to her. I explained to her that we believe she was in an abusive relationship and we would like to help her. She got furious and denied every accusation my sister had made and said my father was a "very good man and amazing father and how dare I say such terrible things about him." The attorney, the family, hired wanted me to testify, as well as my grandparents. This would be my very first time seeing my father face to face since my childhood. Not only that but my other sister was still in total denial and refused to believe my father was abusive. She hated me for doing this to them. The day I walked in that courtroom to take the oath, the tears of betrayal in my mother's eyes were haunting. But I knew I had to do this for their sake. My mother then disowned me for quite some time knowing I was subpoenaed to attend the court hearing. She called and told me I was no longer her daughter, and she was done with me. I fell to the floor hysterically crying because I wasn't expecting such a harsh reaction from her. The months of several court hearings were horrific. My father would constantly harass the family my sister was living with at the time. They filed a restraining order on him. Myself and our family started making many calls to CPS, as well as my sisters' school. Every time CPS would close the case stating my sisters were old enough to take care of themselves and they couldn't help unless my father eventually murders them or puts them in the hospital. My sister started running away, staying with friends as long as possible until my father would call the police, and the police would make my sister return home each time. My father would claim she was a runaway and even after she told the police many times she was very afraid and he was abusive, they told her to "stop misbehaving and listen to her father." Sadly, a few months into the custody hearing the family decided they were going to send my sister back to my parents because she had "too many behavioral problems." So, I never did get my chance to testify in court, my grandmother was able to testify the history of abuse and neglect from my childhood.

Once my sister returned home, my father decided it would be okay for them to start coming over to our house for the very first time, us going out in public together, coming over for holidays and birthdays. That is when my mother got to see her entire family for the first time in years, and the first time my sisters got to meet our family. And we finally got to all spend Thanksgiving, Christmas and other major holidays together. That is when my other sister that was in denial finally came out with the abuse after my father had pinned her to the bed in anger and left several bruises on her arms. I took pictures of her injuries and made yet another report to CPS, all they offered them was counseling. In which my father forced my mother to cancel, and CPS allowed him to make that call. That is when I would get several calls a day from my sisters, screaming and hysterically crying. Begging me to come get them because they were afraid and he was very drunk and being aggressive. My sisters would even call CPS themselves and beg the intake operator to please send someone to come and help them. I would call 911 each time, and the police would side with my father, who had told them his kids were "wild and out of control and he is disciplining them." I would call the police out there many times for welfare checks as well, in which they told me as long as a child has one bowl of cereal a day then that is enough. My father eventually started to ground my sisters from school. I thought that would finally be what CPS would really see a problem with as if everything else happening wasn't already enough. But every CPS caseworker we got would close the case in a week or two, stating there was nothing they could help with at this time and that I needed to stop calling them. The police started blaming my sisters telling them if they were called out to their house one more time, or if they ran away one more time they would be sending them to juvenile detention. My sisters would still run away many times, escaping to friends' houses trying to seek shelter. My mother was too deep into my father's control to even protect her kids at that point. He would tell my mother to "go to her room" while he handled my sisters. At this time, I really had no idea what else to do, CPS failed us. The police failed us. Who else was left for us to turn to?

I started researching resources for women living in domestic violence. I came across the National Domestic Violence Hotline late one night, saw they were a 24-hour hotline, and I gave them a call. And that was where I found my saving grace. I didn't know who else to turn to but knowing I could call experts in this who could tell me how to handle this, understand my frustrations and letting me vent meant so much to me. I would even say the advocate, who I talked to on a nightly basis, became one of my best friends. To this day I only know her first name, Francesca. But she listened to me for hours, and she truly became a friend to me and someone I could trust. When I wanted to give up, she encouraged me, but also reminded me to take some time for myself and if things get overwhelming in this that it's okay if I need to back away temporarily to catch my breath. At that point, I had started to financially support my mom and sisters. My mother didn't have access to her paychecks because he had control of all the finances, bank accounts and he had also ruined her credit score by taking out loans and not paying them back under her name. I started buying them food, clothes, their school supplies, back to school clothes, basic necessities such as shampoo, razors and other beauty and feminine items. Finding churches and other organizations, they could get food at, help get their bills paid, etc. Friends and co-workers started to donate things as well. I work retail, and I don't have much money as it is. But I decided to put all my own needs on the back-burner to make sure they were safe and taken care of. They knew all they needed to do was call me and tell me what they needed, and I would buy it for them. With the help of the Hotline, it really started to give me a passion and a fire in my heart to learn more on Domestic Violence. I figured if I was going to help my mom, I needed to educate myself further to learn as much about this as I could. I ordered two amazing books on Amazon, "Helping Her Get Free: A Guide For Families And Friends Of Abused Women by Susan Brewster, M.S.S.W." as well as the book, "Why Does He Do That? Inside The Minds of Angry and Controlling Men by Lundy Bancroft." I bought myself some highlighters and started on my path of learning the ins and outs of Domestic Violence.

What I soon realized was that one of the most overlooked forms of domestic violence is Financial abuse, my father was very aggressive, controlling, always yelling, always drunk and has a severe alcohol addiction, which made it all the worse, but wasn't always physically abusive. Financial Abuse is very overlooked because there are no physical signs or injuries. But it is just as detrimental as physical abuse.

And it's one of the many reasons victims feel trapped because they have no financial means of escaping or access to any money to flee. Many times, even if the victim does work, such as my mother did, the abuser was still in control of the money and will not let the victim have any of it. The Hotline put me in contact with some amazing organizations and shelters around the area that my mom could go to for help. Anytime I ever mentioned her being in an abusive relationship or possibly getting help, she would get very angry at me. Eventually, she started being more open to having conversations about it. Many times, she would say she was going to leave him, but she would never actually follow through with it. I told her the day she decided to leave, I would be there. No matter the time or the day. She would call me at work, said she has decided to leave, then would call right back and say never mind. Things got so bad I had to tell most of my managers at work the situation because I would have to make 911 calls, take calls from our CPS caseworkers, etc. It literally consumed my entire life, from my thoughts down to my bank account. Having an advocate from the Hotline to call and talk to was a great way for me to let go of my stress and vent. I knew if I kept it all bottled up, I would soon explode. The first time my mother decided to leave it was an early Saturday morning, around 6am. I got a call from her after a heated, aggressive argument took place between them all. Without no hesitation, my family and I jumped into the car and went and got her and my sisters. I was so excited, this was the day we had hoped for. I took her to the store and bought her a whole new wardrobe, necessities and other things she may need during her stay with us until we figured out what to do and how to get her on her feet. I had printed out the "signs of abuse" section on the National Domestic Violence Hotline's website, including the "power and control wheel." When she arrived at our house, we sat down at the kitchen table and went over the papers.

I had her ask herself all the questions on the paper, such as "Does your partner limit where you go, who you talk to, what you do, etc.?" and many of the things listed, it was clicking in her head that these things were happening. I then got in touch with several shelters around the area that could help her get back on her feet, my mother was not ready for that step, she said she was afraid to go and stay in a shelter. About 2 weeks later I come home from work, and she and my sister were gone, and their things were gone. That's when my grandparents told me she decided to go back to my father. I fell to the floor screaming and shaking and sobbing uncontrollably. I picked up the phone and called The Hotline. I learned from them on average, it takes a victim 5 times of escaping before it actually sticks. I had told them at this point, I couldn't put myself through this any longer. I had to take a step back for a while to regroup myself. I was emotionally and physically drained from not only my job but trying to save my mom and sisters in the process. I went probably about a month without talking to my mother. And slowly started putting myself back into the equation. I kept reminding my mother, there is help out there, and all she needs to do is reach out and take it. That we all loved her and want her to be safe and happy. I started to ease back on how much money I would spend on them, at that point, I saw it may have been a crutch and making my dad's behavior continue since he knew I was taking care of his wife and kids as well as my grandparents were helping out. September

2014 was my mother's high school graduation. An old classmate of hers was going and offered to pay for my mother's ticket. She was very excited to see old friends and finally be able to go out and do something fun. The day of the high school reunion, my father told her she was not allowed to go. So, she decided she wouldn't. I called, texted and did all I could to encourage her to stand up for herself, that she deserved to go and deserved to finally have some fun and not allow him to control her anymore. So, she ran down the highway and hid behind a bush until her friend could come pick her up off the side of the road. My father had started walking down the road looking for her, she stayed hidden until her ride came. And that is when it all started to sink in for her how badly her situation had gotten.

October 2014 another heated argument had happened. This was when it all came to an end. My mother had said she couldn't do this anymore, that she had no more feelings for him. He packed up his things and moved to live with his sister about an hour away. She and my sisters had stayed at their house. A week after their split my mother suddenly got fired from her job of 20 years. Which was the worst case of a woman who had just broken free of domestic violence. She doesn't have a car and no driver's license. So, without my father there anymore, she had no form of transportation. She started to walk everywhere, taking a taxi when she could afford it. She found an amazing job, that was the same job she did have, but this time in the same town they live in! She is now a true survivor of Domestic Violence. She finally broke free at the age of 45! If there is one thing I could say to anyone living in abuse, it's that it doesn't matter how old you are, how long you have been abused or what your situation may be, there is a way out! Don't end up like my mother, 45 years old and finally able to live her life freely. So much about her has changed, from the light in her eyes, down to even having her nails painted. She never got to pamper herself, make herself feel beautiful. All she ever got to do was go to work, and couldn't even enjoy the money she has worked so hard for all these years. She is now able to know what it feels like to have a haircut, to own clothes that actually fit and don't have stains and holes, clothes that aren't hand me downs, being able to talk to anyone anytime she wants and go anywhere she pleases. I am so beyond proud of her and tell her all the time she made the best choice she could ever make for herself and my sisters. She still struggles, emotionally and financially, still does not have a vehicle, but she makes the best of her situation, and will even walk a very far distance to get to her work if she can't afford a taxi that day. My sisters are now 19, and I hope they grow to become strong willed women, and know the way a partner should treat you. They don't belittle you, control your every move, take your money and make you and your children go without.

My mother and I are slowly growing in our relationship, I'm sure we will get there one day. It has definitely been a bumpy road of healing. I got into therapy to heal from all of the traumatic events not only from my childhood but from taking on helping my mother and sisters find freedom. Helping someone get free of abuse can be very overwhelming and emotionally and physically exhausting. I had gone into a very bad depression and was prescribed anti-depressants in which I have now not even had to take with the help of therapy. Domestic Violence truly affects everyone, down to the victims' loved ones such as myself. I put so much of my emotions into it, I had lost myself through the pain. Now that I am starting to heal, there is a lot my mother and I are now learning about each other since he kept her away from not only me but her entire family for 24 years. To now be able to call her whenever I want, see her whenever I want and have them spend holidays with us is an indescribable feeling! I now donate to the Hotline yearly, I feel it's my duty and my way of saying thank you for what this organization has done for me and so many others out there who reach out to them for help! This has become my passion in life, my heart's desire, to bring awareness to Domestic Violence. To inform people abuse is more than just hitting, it can be so much more than that. My mom often used the line of, "Well he hasn't hit me, so it isn't abuse." And to this day I'm still not sure if he ever actually hit her or not. She would lie for him so much just as many victims do. It's so odd that they try to protect the one who has destroyed their life, but that is the cycle of abuse. It is brainwashing the victim and isolating them from positive influences that could possibly help them escape. That is why my father hates me so much. Because he knows all that I was trying to do to help my mom escape. He has blamed this all on her, saying she has split up his family and destroyed their marriage. He will not take responsibility for any of his actions. And that is exactly what abusers do. They see no fault in their behavior and will place the blame on anyone or anything and make excuses. What he does not realize is HE is the one that destroyed his family and his marriage. HE is the one to blame for all that has happened. But he still plays the victim and says, "I don't know why nobody likes me, nobody knows me so how can they judge me." We do not have to know him on a personal level to know what he has done is not okay and needs to be stopped!

I now share my story in huge ways globally. Domestic Violence has been in my family since the 1920s, from generation to generation. I am the first person in my family to finally speak out and break the cycle. I speak for the ones in my family who no longer are on this earth, who never had the chance to raise their voice and break free. And for the ones still living, who are still looking for their voice and courage to share their story. I am the one who decided enough is enough, and our family will no longer continue this cycle. Our voices and stories must be heard. We must break the silence. Because of that, I was approached by The National Domestic Violence Hotline to share my story for their annual Giving campaign they have every December in 2016. I was invited to attend their 20th Anniversary Banquet on February 14th, 2016 in Austin, TX. A quote from my article was featured in the night's event. I was able to meet the staff at The Hotline, as well as the amazing CEO of The Hotline, Katie Ray-Jones. She has said my story is an inspiration to so many. My life story even has taken me to the Nation's Capital! I was selected by the White House administration to attend the very first ever United State Of Women Summit in Washington, D.C. on June 14th, 2016. An event where women from all over the world gathered with former President Barack Obama and Former First Lady Michelle Obama, Oprah, and many other celebrities all there to discuss female empowerment and issues women face daily, one being violence against women. My local news, Fox 4 DFW, got word of my selection and came out to my house to interview me for my own segment. A GoFundMe page was set up for me to help fund my trip, not only was $700 raised by strangers who saw me on the news and friends of mine to totally cover my hotel stay, but a dear friend of mine even completely covered my airfare! Making this amazing, once in a lifetime opportunity possible for me! With these opportunities, I have been able to communicate with women from all around the world and help them find freedom. They tell me I am their inspiration and what they don't realize is, THEY are my inspiration! Their courage, their bravery, their strength, is what inspires me and keeps me going and passionate about what I do. And the reason why I will no longer let anyone silence me ever again! People need to hear about these things!

We must empower victims. If we don't, who else will be able to get to them? It's not ever an "it's none of my business" or "Why doesn't she just leave?" It is so much deeper and more psychological than anyone could ever understand. We must continue to fight for a change in our justice system when it comes to Child Protective Services as well as how law enforcement handles domestic violence cases. Too many families are left without the help they need due to CPS and the police not doing what is necessary to protect abuse victims and their children. That is why I know this is what I am meant to do in life. I can use my story to raise awareness. If it wasn't for my faith and all my family and friends who have helped me get through these past few years, I don't know how I would have gotten through it! I hope with my story, I can reach victims and the friends and families of victims worldwide, that it is NEVER too late to escape the life of abuse and control. All you need to do is be brave, know that you deserve better than the life you have been living, and reach out for help!

SURVIVOR TALK
Building Self-Confidence

Don't compare yourself to others. You are not someone else. You have a unique skillset and unique mind. Never compare yourself with others. You only need to be better than who you were.

Don't strive for perfection. Perfection should never be the goal. As the quote says, "Perfection is the enemy of good." Striving for perfection you can "never" reach only disillusions and depresses you. Never go for perfection go for "good enough" or "better than average."

Positive self-talk. What you say matters. You can be your biggest critic or your own best supporter.

Focus on the things you can change. There are enough things you can change that you should never worry about the things you can't. Focus on those simple changes that have a big impact in your life.

Do the things you enjoy. Life is for living. When you go out and enjoy life you have fun. Fun and happiness are a natural state that build happiness, and happiness and contentment in turn work to build confidence.

Don't beat yourself up over a mistake. Everyone makes mistakes. If you make a mistake just admit it. Fix it, and move on.

Celebrate the small stuff. Start small and work your way up, gaining confidence the whole way. The best progress is done through small steps, not through massive leaps and bounds.

Be considerate of others. Being helpful to others not only makes them feel better, but it will also make you feel better.

Surround yourself with supportive people. Motivational speaker Jim Rohn famously said, "you are the average of the five people you spend the most time with". So, you want to spend time with people who are confident, supportive and kind, so that you will find yourself reflecting these traits.

n.d. 7 September 2017.
<http://www.developgoodhabits.com/affirmations-self-esteem-confidence/>.

It's hard to deal with injuries mentally, but think of it as a new beginning. We can't change what happened, so we focus on healing and becoming stronger than before.
~Wounds to Wisdom

Chapter Eight

LABOR DAY
By April Kelley

To appoint unto them that mourn in Zion, to give unto them beauty for ashes, the oil of joy for mourning, the garment of praise for the spirit of heaviness; that they might be called trees of righteousness, the planting of the Lord, that he might be glorified." -Isaiah 61:3

How did I get here is the question that I asked myself while looking in the mirror. I worked really hard to become the woman in the mirror looking back at me. I am not perfect but I finally feel complete. I can finally say that I love me and I am proud of me, as my mind reflects on the hardships that it took for me to get here. I have always been a happy and cheerful person on the outside, but it took a while for me to feel it on the inside. I have always had a passion for helping others to become successful and succeed at their goals; however, they never saw the brokenness that was inside of me.

To tell you a little about myself, I am a Beauty/Pageant Queen of many titles, senior superlative in high school (best dressed). I started reading at the age of 3 and talking at the age of 6 months. I graduated with honors when attaining both a bachelor and master's degree, yet I wasn't smart enough to leave the man who was abusing me. The most painful memory that continues to burn in my heart is memories of my mornings.

Mornings were important in my family. When I was a child my parents were excited to wake my brother and I up in the mornings. My mom loved to cook breakfast for us. We hardly ever ate cereal. I was used to praying in the mornings and spending alone time with God. My mornings turned from happiness to sadness. After and during the abuse I remember that it took me approximately 3 hours to get dressed for work. I cried for hours, blaming myself for my x-fiancé leaving me and blaming myself that my x-boyfriend stopped texting me and calling me. Everything seemed to happen around Labor Day! When I started healing from my x-fiancé (James), my x boyfriend (Paul) began to hurt me. My x-fiancé used to text me in the mornings and call me in the mornings to check on me. I looked forward to starting my day hearing his voice. I looked forward to praying with him in the mornings. When he left me, I felt a void in my heart that I had never felt before. I was hurt to my core. It took several people calling me in the mornings to help me start my day. My mom used to tell me, "April get up and push, you can do this!" I can recall all of the conversations that I had with Trixy, Nichole, Kristle, Aunt Denise, Aunt Pat, Brian, Rayshawn, my god mother Betty, and LaToya. After I finally got the strength to get up and start my day, I cried on the way to work and I had to call Leah, Angela, Gwen, Velma, or Glynetta to help me get through my afternoon. Life was so difficult and it hurt really bad. There were so many people praying for me and cheering me on.

My x-fiancé' was my best friend. We went to college together and I could not picture life without him. He gave me the proposal of my dreams! Things were good between us but we had our dark moments. A few months into our engagement things began to calm down between us, so I thought. He came to visit me for Labor Day Weekend. I was sexually assaulted and lost my virginity Labor Day weekend. My first fiancé broke up with me Labor Day Weekend, etc... As you can see, Labor Day Weekends are not good to me. I began to hate Labor Day. When James got back to his home he called me to tell me that he wanted to be my friend. He said that we needed to go back to how we used to be while in college. His idea was for us to go to counseling and see if we can come back together again. I was devastated. I began to scream and cried out to God.

My first fiancé treated me like Gold but I did not know how to treat him because I had just gotten sexually assaulted. I just wanted someone to treat me right and not leave me! I went to counseling to become a better person and try to heal. While I was in counseling, I later found out that he was with another woman and had moved on. During this time, I prayed because I wanted him back. I just knew he was the man for me. God answered my prayers. we got back together and got back engaged in January. In April, he told me that his ex-girlfriend was pregnant and he disappeared in June. I was left again with a broken lonely heart.

Then all of a sudden, he popped up! His name was Paul! He was handsome and he was so concerned about everything that I'd been through. He wanted to know why my mornings were so hard. He wanted to know how could he fix my problems. Everyone at my church told me that Paul was the one for me! My parents loved him too. Paul would make me feel like I was the only one in the world. I sent Paul a picture of me and he replied that he needed to take me shopping. I tried to explain to him that I did not need to go shopping. He said, "Yes, every lady needs new attire. When I come to visit you next week we are going shopping". The following week Paul showed up at my doorstep. I began to get scared because things were moving at a much faster pace than I was used to. Paul was talking about marriage on our first date. I kept telling him that he needed to court me and get to know me a little better. On our first date, we stopped by an outlet mall and Paul insisted on purchasing clothes for me. I begged him not to and I tried to explain to him that he was making me feel uncomfortable. I was used to fussing and fighting with James and I did not have any fight left in me, so I went into the dressing room and complied with what he asked me to do.

Paul seemed to be concerned about my well-being. He was concerned about what I wanted to accomplish and achieve in life. He was very concerned about how my x-fiancé treated me. He wanted to know why I had abandonment issues and why I felt abandoned by my x-fiancé. I poured my heart out to Paul and I wanted him to know everything about my past. I felt like he was genuine and that he cared. Paul promised me that he would never make me cry, he assured me that I was safe because I was with him now. He promised me that world. He promised that if I gave him a chance that he would show me love that I'd never seen before. I was very careful with Paul and I wanted to take my time with him because I was still in love with James. I used to tell him that I felt like James was my husband and that he would come back to me. Paul assured me that James would never come back and that he left me so that I could move on. He told me that James really didn't love me because love doesn't leave! I remember he shared with me that God's blessings add riches to your life and not any sorrow. He started quoting scriptures to try to make me feel better, but my heart was telling me different.

After two weeks of trying to convince Paul of being my friend and allowing me to heal he got very upset and cut me off. He cut me off in a way that I had never seen before. He had so much anger in his heart and aggravation toward me. Once again, I felt like everything was my fault.

My parents asked me to contact him and tell him how I felt and talk to him and pray. I began to pray and I called Kristle (my prayer partner) and she began to pray with me too. We were excited because we knew that in two weeks I would see Paul at our church conference. We had two weeks to pray for him to come back. I felt like I needed to pray because it was obvious that I did not know what was best for me. I needed to listen to everyone else. They were telling me that he was a great man of God and that he would be a great husband to me. My heart still loved James, but my mind was telling me maybe I should try to move on.

Two weeks had come and Paul and I ran into each other during our church conference. I said, Paul why did you do that? Why were you so mean to me? This is not what our church teaches and your actions are not how a Godly man is supposed to treat a woman. He did not know what to say. He asked me if I could meet him somewhere so that we could talk. When we met up later that evening, he had roses and a card in his hands. I was shocked and happy that he wanted to chat over what happened. He apologized to me and told me that he did not mean what he said. He said, "When I told you that I was weighing my options, it was because I was angry with you. I was selfish and I am sorry. You are correct, I was not supposed to cut you off like that. I was cutting grass at the church." I cut him off and said, no you were being mean and selfish. The only reason we are talking is because everyone keeps telling me to give you a chance and I am trying but you have to be patient with me. He agreed to be patient and I told him that we could be friends.

Time passed and Paul started talking to me about relocating to Atlanta. He asked me how did I feel about having children. I expressed to him that I did not really care about having children because he had his children and grandchildren. He started to say all of the right things and I felt on top of the world but I still felt empty inside. I did not have the "butterflies" that I had when I dated James.

Paul came to visit and wanted to take me to the Myrtle Beach. He used to rent luxury cars when he came to visit. We stopped by my parents' house on the way to the beach and enjoyed our ride. I felt like this was the perfect time for me to open up and tell him about me.

I explained to Paul that I was sexually assaulted by 3 men. I started to tell him how hard it is for me to trust men and how hard it is for me to be with someone sexually. I told him that I did not want to have sex before marriage. I talked to Paul about James. He seemed very concerned about James and why James left me. I told Paul that I was not sure why James left me but James loved me. I started going on and on about James and the things that we used to do. I could not understand why he left. Paul started telling me that James was not in love with me and he did not care about me. Paul said that James was with another woman and had moved on. He said, "honey that's what men do. We move on". I began to feel the tears forming in my eyes. Paul said,

"But it's ok because I am here now. I will be here by your side. You don't need him now. All you need is me". I said but James promised me that he loved me and that he was going to marry me. He said, "He lied to you sweetie. Do you see where he is now, has he called to check on you, has he texted you? A real man will check on his lady. Don't worry about him. I am going to be patient and love you. You are pulling on my heart strings." I started to get so confused because I had just met him and he was in love already. Maybe he was right. Maybe James was not into me anymore. He got another lady pregnant so why am I waiting on him?

When we arrived at the Beach house Paul wanted to come into my room. I told him that I did not feel comfortable with him coming into my room because we weren't married. Paul came into my room and started explaining to me why we needed to sleep together. He got the Bible to further explain to me with scriptures that I was safe with him and it was ok for us to sleep together. He said, "I am planning to marry you so we can have sex." He began to use the information that I shared with him about being assaulted sexually against me. I was shaking and scared because since I'd been sexually assaulted I no longer knew how to say NO! I asked him to leave out of my room and please give me a moment to think. He slammed the door and I got into the shower.

When I got out of the shower there were eggs, plates, cups, milk, etc. everywhere. He had thrown all of the breakfast food that I'd just cooked all over the floors and walls. He was trying to clean it up before I saw it. I asked him very calmly, what happened to the eggs? He said, "I will buy some more. Don't ask." I was very hurt and scared. This was the first day that I knew I needed to "tread lightly" with Paul. For the rest of the trip my answers to Paul were everything that he wanted to hear. I felt very uncomfortable inside but I knew I could not tell him about it because this would only cause us to have more issues. I did not want him to blow up on me like James.

James used to go from 0-600 in 60 seconds! He had a temper on him and a cold attitude to match. Paul knew that I was scared of men when they expressed their anger towards me. James knew that anger would either make me retaliate or shut down. I walked into the room and prayed to God asking him to help me. I remember asking God was I the problem and if I was to please show me myself. Paul knocked on the door and told me that we needed to go to the outlet mall tomorrow so that I could get something nice. I said, I really don't want you spending any money. He said with a smile, "well you spend your money and I pay you back." I let out a sigh because I really did not want to try on clothes for him like I did during his first visit. He made me try on clothes, model the clothes while he sat with his legs crossed looking at me like I was a piece of meat. I hated that feeling that I got the first time we went shopping and I did not want to feel it again; however, I better tell him what he wanted to hear because I didn't want to end up like the eggs that were thrown this morning.

The next day we went to the outlet mall and spent over $3,000. I kept telling him that I did not need anything. Paul said, "Remember you are purchasing and I am just paying you back." He purchased a few things with his credit card, and I tried to make the best out of this situation. On the way home, I spoke to Paul openly about feeling uncomfortable and I just wanted him to get to know me first. I told him that I could tell that he was used to buying his women. I explained to him that I was not the type of woman that could be brought. He said, "Did James buy you gifts and treat you like I just treated you?" I replied No, but he used to get me gifts every now and then. He started chuckling, "A woman of your caliber needs to be wined and dined with gifts often." I asked, even if I feel uncomfortable? I started to see his body language change. I grabbed his hand and said, never mind. Thank you.

Paul began to tell me how he was going to pay me back by helping to pay my bills; however, when it was time for the bills to be paid he got upset with me and would not answer my phone calls. When I finally got him on the phone 3 days later, he said that he ignored me because I did not answer him properly when he called met the last time. I was so confused and then it dawned on me that when he called and said, "hey what are you doing? I missed you talking to you today." I replied that I was watching Scandal. He got furious. He said that I should have said that I missed him too. I tried to explain to him that I did miss him; however I was answering the first part of the question and that was... "What are you doing"? He began to tell me how I cared more about Scandal than I cared about him. This turned into an argument, but the difference between Paul and James is that Paul never ever raised his voice, but because I was so used to James, I did all of the screaming and yelling. Paul said very calmly, "Since you did not miss me, I did not talk to you for a few days until you missed me". At this time, my lights were disconnected because I went shopping with my light bill money. Paul promised to pay me back. This was only the first of many shopping trips where I listened to Paul, overspent, he got upset, cut me off, and bills did not get paid; however, every time he came back. He was bearing gifts and more gifts! This was the first of the Roller Coaster Ride with Paul!

Paul continued to use the Bible as a means to manipulate me throughout our entire relationship. I was never "Godly, Saved, or Virtuous" enough. Paul used my past and the things that I'd been through against me. I told Paul everything about me because he and I were in the same religion and I thought I could trust him. I learned very quickly that Paul played a lot of mind games. As long as I complied to his demands, and commands he would call me his honey and baby, but when I did not do what he wanted me to do I got cut completely off. Paul did not want me to sing with the group that I used to sing with because the group spoke in tongues and believed differently than we were taught. He used to tell me that did not want me hanging out with my choir friends any more.

One day I was out with my friends and Paul called me to tell me that he did not think we should date any more. He said that I don't listen to him and I have a lot of issues that I need to take care of. Every two days he would break up with me if I did not do what he wanted me to do. He was aware of the abandonment issues that I had from dating James. Paul played upon my emotions all the time. I remember begging and crying for him to not leave me. He chuckled and said very calmly and quietly that he would try to stay but I needed to be a "Godly young lady and do things right." Within seconds he was asking me to make him happy and send him nude photos of me. I to myself, is this what "being Godly and Holy" means? Asking for nude pictures of me! However, I had to comply or I would get in trouble or cut off. I texted my best friend who knew how to find pictures that might be me on the internet. We used to do this all the time back in the day! We cropped the heads off the ladies and I sent them to Paul. He replied, "I love your body and thanks for the pictures. You just made my night". I thought to myself, you are so crazy! That is not me! My best friend and I got caught one day sending these pictures out! We sent them to the wrong people on accident and someone actually thought that it was me. I laughed so hard! It feels good to know a secret that only you know! It was a rule of ours to never send pictures of ourselves! I made Paul happy by sending pictures, answering yes sir to him, and trying to be the virtuous woman that HE wanted me to be and not God. He made me happy by staying around as my "friend" and buying things. Eventually I finally gave in to receiving gifts from him. The gifts got more and more expensive as the time went on. We began to talk about marriage. I tried to mention James (my x-fiancé') less and less when we talked but it was hard. The butterflies that I used to feel were missing. Paul did not yell at me like James did. He never threw things at me like James did, but Paul was not the Godly man that he was supposed to be. He broke up with me every other day when I did not comply to him.

I was very excited to go to the mall with Paul. I told him that I wanted to purchase a bracelet to match my necklace. I picked out two bracelets and when I was not looking Paul purchased them for me. I told him that I wanted to purchase the bracelets for myself. He begged me to let him do it and treat me. He said that I could treat him in the men's store. I thought we were finally moving in a good direction. We started walking upstairs to the men's store and a younger man looked at me and said hi, I spoke and kept walking. Paul got very angry and accused me of flirting with this guy. He tried to leave me at the mall. I was pleading with him that I did not want that other man. Paul said, "You are looking at him because he is closer to your age." I spent a lot of time convincing Paul that age was not a factor for us, but he spent a lot of time getting angry with me and reminding me that I was too immature. He told me that I was not being a Godly woman looking at other men. While walking to the car I apologized and told him that I would not look at men anymore. I begged him to please take me home. I told him that I could not find another ride. I told him all the things that would make him happy. When I got in the car, I looked out of the window and cried silently to myself. I prayed to God that the pain would go away. This roller coaster ride was too much for me.

I can recall more times that Paul got angry with me. Paul's anger scared me, because it was not loud, it was quiet and calm. One day in particular, I did not answer the phone when he called; he left a terrible message on my voice mail. When I called him back and told him I was in the shower and noticed that I missed his call, he said, "Baby don't check the message that I left you. I thought you were ignoring my calls. Next time take me with you to the shower." He stared laughing trying to make light of the situation but I knew I needed to get out of this relationship.

I eventually told Paul that he did not love me because James had shown me more love than he ever showed me. I told him that he had a problem being told No! He needed to work on something's within himself before he would be ready to be in a relationship. This was when the light bulb went off and Paul apologized for his behavior. He texted me and told me that he had no idea that he was abusing me emotionally until I pointed everything out to him. He told me that if I never speak to him again, he would understand.

Eventually Paul broke up with me and he sent me a terrible text message after I tried to get him back. I was only trying to get him back because I thought that maybe I was the problem. Remembering James never said that I did anything right, so at this point I needed to stop making men mad at me.

The emotional and spiritual abuse was revealed to my parents and brother and they were not happy. Paul used to break up with me every other day over everything that I did. He used to tell me that I was not mature enough for him; he changed his mind he will never move to Atlanta, he will never have children with me; he has grandchildren and has accomplished a lot in his life. He made me feel like I was less of a woman because I was younger than he was. My mind began to reminisce on the fun times that I had with James but there were dark times as well.

I remember like it was yesterday, I was in the shower and James knocked on the door and told me that he needed to talk to me about something very important. Later on, he asked me if I was cheating on him. He wanted to know who I went to see when I went back to my hometown. I was thinking, why is he asking me this and where is he going with this. I began to get scared and I told him that I went to see some friends. He said yea but did you sleep with your friends? I told him that I did not sleep with anyone and I asked him why did he need to know. Immediately he became furious with me. He started to yell and scream at me. He accused me of everything. I called my mother on the phone and told her what was going on. My dad spoke with both of us on the phone and tried to help calm the situation. James was slamming doors and threatening to leave me. He started telling me that I really did not love him and care. I was shaking and crying begging him to stay. My insides felt like they were going to fall out of my body. I couldn't believe that this would cause him to get so angry. That was the beginning of our "not so good" situations. During this time both of our immediate family were involved. Everyone believed in us and wanted to see us make it.

My mind reflects on the day that, James got so angry with me that he grabbed my dog and would not give her back to me. The dog was shaking and crying. She got so upset that she urinated on the floor. I did not know and I came downstairs and slipped and fell. I hit my hand and arm on the cabinet to stop my head from hitting the hardwood floor. He continued to fuss and yell at me. I started to tell him in a calm voice that I needed to go to the hospital. His response was, "whatever man, you love to play the victim card" and he continued to fuss at me. I packed my things and drove myself to the hospital. I left him at my house fussing at me. He found out what hospital I was at and came to the ER and continued to fuss and ask me questions. I kept telling him that this was not the place nor the time to do this. I really did not feel like arguing with him. I was mentally exhausted. I could not wrap myself around why I was such a "bad person" in his eyes. This was the day that I learned about James cold heart and spirit.

In both relationships, I used to cry often and try to explain myself. I always wondered why things were my fault. I tried often to make them happy. Sometimes I sacrificed who I was and what made me happy, but it seemed as though I was always failing in the relationship arena. The emotional abuse and up and down roller coaster ride was too much for me to handle. Before all of this began, I was in a good relationship, but he left me Labor Day Weekend through a text message. He had a "one night stand" before we started dating and she was pregnant, so he wanted to do the right thing by her. It was official that I hated Labor Day!

I learned a lot from dating Paul and James. I had to take some time to heal and forgive! I forgave myself for allowing April/ME to go through all of that mess! I forgave Paul for spiritually abusing me and manipulating me through the Bible and religion, I forgave James for abandoning me, having babies with another woman. I forgave the men who sexually assaulted me and took my innocence from me; I forgave anyone who has called me a liar (because my story kept changing when I was confused). I forgave my heart for loving the wrong people unconditionally! After I forgave, I allowed God to heal me completely and take away all scars, so there will be no residue. I began to love on me unconditionally and invest in me. I now do everything that makes me happy without man's permission! Getting a man was never hard to do, but walking away was. My mentor (Tamiko) challenged me to a 30-day man fast that turned into a 180-day man fast! I am no longer the same person. I allowed God to turn my ashes into his beauty. No longer a victim but a victor! I also fasted and prayed that the Labor Day "Curse" would be completely removed! I accepted the peace of Jehovah Shalom and asked God to remove all FEARS that are contributed to Labor Day! To be continued...

SURVIVOR TALK
Forgiveness Prayer

Dear God, please help me to forgive. Please help me to be willing to release old grievances. Please help me to cleanse my mind, body, and soul of old stored up anger. Please help me to move past the focus upon earthly egos, and to see the big picture. And please help me to stop repeating the pattern of attracting hurtful relationships and situations. Please protect me from anyone who would take advantage of me or betray me in any way. Amen

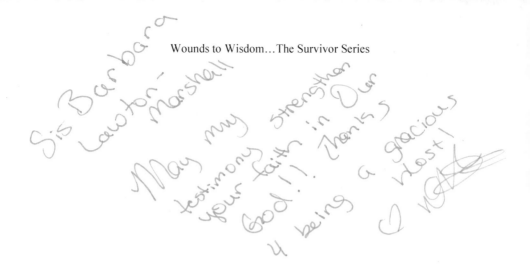

Sis Barbara Lawton-Marshall

May may testimony strengthen your faith in Our God!!! Thanks 4 being a gracious host! ♡

Your life experiences help you to understand the positive and negative influences that mold your values and behaviors.
~Wounds to Wisdom

Chapter Nine

BY GRACE
By Duntenia Fitts

Survival was my only hope, success my only revenge.
~Patricia Cornwell

I was born in Los Angeles California. The youngest of all my siblings, I remember my older sister telling me that I was an "oops" baby because my parents had not planned on having more kids. My parents separated when I was only six months old, and my mother decided to move us back to Rochester New York. As a young girl, I lived in housing projects called Van Aucker. I never knew that I used to live in the projects, I just thought a neighborhood that I grew up in with my friends. I thought it was the best place ever! My favorite show to watch in the 80s was Jem and the Holograms and Pee Wee Herman on Saturday mornings. I was enrolled in Dance Patrol where I took up ballet, played the flute and danced in parades. In my eyes, I had the best life that anybody could ask for. As a child growing up in those conditions, I didn't have the luxury of knowing that there was a life outside of the projects. We were our own community. My school, my teachers, friends, and family were from the west side of Rochester New York.

I remember one night going grocery shopping with my mom at one of the best Supermarkets called Wegmans. My mom was getting lots of groceries. I wondered what would come of this and why she was saying yes to everything I asked for. She let me get anything in the store I asked for.

The next morning, I woke up for school tired and sleepy from staying up late, sneaking to watch Johnny Carson On the Tonight Show. I woke up weary my pink pajamas and noticed that my TV had been turned off. As I walked into the living room, I saw a tall, dark skinned man. I was about nine years old at this time. As I stared at the man, I immediately knew, without a shadow of a doubt that this was my father. The first thing he said to me was "hello little lady." I said hi as I wiped my eyes. My parents asked me if I knew who he was. I said, "yeah my father!" And they laughed. I thought it would be so great to have a dad in the house because I always imagined that my dad would be like Bill Cosby. A short time later, I realized that my dad was not like Bill Cosby. He was more like David Ruffin.

During this time, I was raised like an only child because my other siblings were all adults. There were nights when my father would come home drunk, and my parents would end up arguing all night. They would be yelling and screaming so loud that it would wake me up.

I was ten years old and began wetting the bed like a baby. Back then I didn't know why I was doing it, but now that I am aware that it was due to the amount of anxiety that I was facing. I wasn't used to waking up to heavy arguments every night. But it had now become routine.

During the day, we would still attend all of our church functions, my school functions, and extracurricular activities. But once we got home, my dreams of what I've always thought I could be were shattered. With my dad being in the household, I began to look at life differently. It was no longer this make-believe, imaginative life where I could be anything

I wanted to be because my father had made it clear in more ways than one that the dreams that I had were not possible. He had a voice out of this world. But I had come to the conclusion that all he could do was sing well, tell funny stories when he was in the mood, and protect me if someone else tried to do anything bad to me.

While sitting in the bath tub one day, I overheard my father (I think he had been drinking) say to my mom, "you know I didn't want her anyway, I didn't want any more kids." At that moment, I felt as if life was no longer full of fun possibilities or hope. I believed from that day on; I was forever changed.

Not long after that, my mom and I moved to Vegas with my father. I remember going to a school where I was the only black person in my class. The teacher appeared to be very nice in the beginning, but as the time when on, things changed. I had never really experienced prejudice or racism before until now. There was a time when my teacher had me sit in the middle of the class. She told the entire class to point at me and laugh. It was such a humiliating experience. I remember on several occasions where she told the class to do mean things to me, and the kids will come outside during recess to tell me they were sorry and that they would never do it again.

I never told my parents because we were going through so much at the time that I didn't even think it mattered. There were some days when we were staying at a hotel some days we were homeless. Two years later we finally move back to Rochester. Although I was happy, there was an innocence that had left me. I wasn't the same anymore. I went back to the same school and got to be around familiar people, but my confidence and self-esteem were gone.

Throughout the years my parents would get back together then break up again. Get back together, then break up again, and again. During my teenage years, the only thing that kept me sane was the fact that God allowed me to be accepted into the school of the arts for High School. Being around other artistic, talented kids like me re-sparked my imagination to dream again. High school was a place where I could Escape.

I graduated high school at the age of 17 and went straight to college. That next year my parents got back together again. My father and I had a falling out on my 18th birthday over a VCR. He told me to get out and not to come back because I didn't live there anymore. So, I ended up staying with some friends and there until finally, me and three other girls became roommates. It was during this time that I met a guy 20 years older than me. He took an interest in me and was always there when I needed him for money, food, clothes or whatever I was in need of at that time.

I didn't think much of it, but I was being groomed into a relationship. During this relationship, I didn't want for anything, but I was getting further and further behind in my studies and was no longer interested in school. I was going shopping on trips and whatever I wanted I got. As I got older and began to mature, I got bored with it all. Five years had passed, and I had absolutely nothing to show for it, besides material things.

This was the first time a guy hit me. He knew I was maturing and no longer was interested in him or his material possessions. I was evolving as a woman, and it showed! In order to physically and mentally get away from hell, I move to Atlanta. While I was in Atlanta, I was with my daughter's father. Our relationship didn't work out, so I went back home to Rochester, New York.

Back home in Rochester, I began going out with friends. On the weekends, I'd go to the local bars and clubs. There was this one neighborhood bar located on the West Side that everybody went to. That was the place to be. You could eat, drink, see everyone you grew up, and just chill out. For the most part, everyone knew each other, especially if you lived on the west side.

I've always had a thing for bad boys, but I never thought this particular incident would change my life forever. It came to my attention that one particular guy liked me but I never really paid him any attention because he was just a part of the crew that we hung out with at the bar. I had a home girl who was dating the guy's cousin out of this particular crew and anytime they knew it was going to be drama they would alert my home girl and tell us to get out of the club. Time goes by, and we all continue to hang out. My home girl brought it to my attention again that this particular guy liked me. This time I was open to it. Little did I know we would later have a son together. I thought that this relationship would go far because I like I said before, we were just friends that hung out with the same crew. But after spending time with him for a while, I saw that he had a really great heart. We would just sit and talk about everything. Things that he and I went through as little kids, our families, life goals and how we both had daddy issues. I was really shocked to find out that he was such a sweetheart.

One particular time, my daughter was in the south visiting her dad and his family. They had gotten used to me flying my daughter down there for free because I was a flight attendant and this time around they didn't want to help me pay for a ticket. Well, my new-found friend offered to fly my daughter down south and told me not to worry about anything. He told me that if I were going to be with him, he would always make sure that my daughter and I were taken care of. And he did just that!

As time went on, I began to notice some red flags. I said to my home girl, "I know I like hood dudes, but these dudes are too Hood." She looked at me, and said, "girl I was thinking the same thing." We then laughed about it, not knowing how deep it would get.

I can remember the first time he put his hands on me. He had been drinking Remy Martin and came to my house. He started yelling at me telling me that I thought I was all of that and then began calling me out my name. Now being who I am, (I'm No Angel, and I definitely have a mouth that has gotten me into a lot of trouble) I began to argue back with him and call him out his name as well. All of a sudden, he ran over to me and grabbed me by my neck. He started choking me to the floor. I remember the look on his face. It was as if he turned into something totally different. I couldn't breathe... I thought that he would see the look on my face and realize that he was going too far. But he didn't stop. I remember seeing all white at one point. Then he finally let go. At that moment, I knew that dating him was a mistake. After that incident, I didn't talk to him. He called a couple of times, but I didn't answer.

A couple of months went by, and I heard that he had gotten shot. I felt so bad because it made me think of an ex-boyfriend who I didn't talk to after he tried to reach out, but it was too late. I didn't want this same thing to happen because I knew how quickly people lost their lives from where I was from. I immediately called his grandmother's house to see if he was okay and if he wanted anything to eat. He asked me to bring him some McDonald's, and I did. This marked the beginning of our "real relationship."

Throughout the course of our relationship, he was abusive. I can't even count how many times I was in the hospital for either a concussion, eye damage, and just everything you can imagine. I thought I could handle it. Everyone that I knew saw the bad side of him, but I saw the good side. The good side that prayed with me and the good side that told me he had never been to church before other than when he was a real little kid and coming to church with me. I saw the good side of him taking care of my daughter, and when people and friends and family would turn their backs on me or be hating, he was there. I honestly felt that this person who was physically hurting me still had my back in other areas.

During this relationship of confusion, I got pregnant. I contemplated if I was going to have my child, his child because I didn't want to bring a kid into a relationship that I knew wasn't going to work out. I actually went to the abortion clinic. Prior to that, the Holy Spirit had been dealing with me about how it hurts God when women have abortions. But, I figured since I was already living in sin, what was one more sin going to do.

My boyfriend told me that he knew I was thinking about having an abortion. He told me that if I ever killed his baby, he was going to kill me. I didn't believe he would intentionally kill me, but it could happen by accident from one of his black out moments when fighting me. I went back to the abortion clinic, and the doctor told me that this time they were going to start the process while I was there because I didn't come back to do the full abortion l was supposed to. I thought that was very strange. As she was doing the sonogram, I saw the baby

Breathe In and Out. My daughter was with me, who was three at the time. She said, "is that the baby?" I said "yes!" Then I told the doctor that I changed my mind. She made a smart remark causing us to exchange words. That was my cue to leave.

I knew it wasn't meant for me to have an abortion. Throughout my pregnancy, my boyfriend didn't really fight me. There was a time when he pulled my hair and another time when he choked me. He didn't fight me like all of the other times because he really wanted his son to be born. Although he had other kids, he wanted to name our son after him. He really wanted this baby.

I didn't have a happy pregnancy at all. He was cheating on me with different girls. I will go up on the block where he hung out to confront him and go off. He still wouldn't fight me because he didn't want me to lose the baby.

After the baby was born, the calm side of him came back out. I was able to sleep throughout the night because he would stay up taking care of the baby. The only time he would wake me up, was for me to feed the baby. He really loved him.

As time went on, I couldn't take it anymore. He was single, and in the streets, all while trying to keep a lid on me. I have always been the type to say, "I can show you better than I can tell you." I was determined to let him know that just because I had two kids, I was not going to stop my life. I began to go back out to the clubs and party with my friends on the weekend. I would just try to avoid the club's that I knew he was going to be at. As time went on, we broke up and got back together about 100 times. This time I thought we really were broken up for good because we hadn't talked in a month. He would watch the baby when I went to work, but as far as a relationship, we were not together.

I decided to go on a double date with one of my friends to a really nice spot. It was hard to find nice little spots in Rochester because someone was always doing something stupid to have it closed down. So, we were at this nice little spot with these two nice guys having a nice time when my boyfriend's cousins and homeboys came in the club. They saw us having a nice time. Now, even though we were broken up, his crew felt like they wanted to mess up my night. So, one came up to me and asked me what I was doing with these funny dudes and just being really rude. They finally call him, (which I knew they would do) and tell him to come up to the club. At this time, I had a restraining order against him. When he came into the club, he came straight up to me and said, "come on let me buy you a drink!" I was like, no thank you; I don't want to drink. He was like, "you want me to start acting up in the club?" I was trying to prevent any type of commotion because I know him and his crew loves commotion.

Not only do I think about my safety, but I'm thinking about the safety of the people I'm with. So, I tell the security guard that I have a restraining order against my son's dad and that he is harassing me. I asked the security guard to please, either make them leave or at least keep an eye on me.

While talking to the security guard, my boyfriend's cousin gave the security guard a look to intimidate him. He also intimidated the guys. The security guard told me to hide in the bathroom. I had to tell a female security guard, who is some off-duty police what was going on, and she made my son's dad leave.

While leaving the club, his crew was outside. They were talking junk to the guys, just being really mean, rude and immature. I got dropped off at home. While going in my door, I see someone run up to me. It was my son's dad. He slammed me on the ground, kicked me, and punched me. I tried to fight back, but he fought even harder. He picked up the steel garbage can and hit me in the face with it, which broke half of my tooth off. It was devastating, to say the least. I could hear the sirens coming. He ran off and got in the car. (Mind you he was in another girl's car doing all of this). My neighbors came outside to check on me after he pulled off. The police and ambulance came and took me to the hospital. It was a really bad, bloody night of many. After this situation, I was so done! I mean that's how I'm known, by my smile. So, for him to do this to me, it was just hurtful, to say the least. Everyone knows me from my smile, and you have made it your business to do to make me ugly!

During the following weeks, he was apologetic. He wrote a letter saying that he didn't know what was wrong with him and that he wanted help. I'm not the first female that he has abused. Somewhere in the back of my mind, I thought that I was keeping the peace by staying.

I remember laying on my couch one. I was just tired. I remember God speaking to me and telling me that if He couldn't change him, what makes you think you can. All of a sudden, I felt this Supernatural feeling of some arms holding and hugging me, then I fell asleep. I will never forget that night.

As time went on, I finally got accepted into the nursing program that I had been trying to get into for four years. I was so excited! My boyfriend was laying in the bed as I was calling everyone telling them that I was accepted. He looked at me and said "would you be quiet, I'm trying to sleep. Nobody cares about that stupid nursing school." As bad as the last fight we had, it got worse and happened more frequently after being accepted into nursing school.

The last fight happened after he had been drinking for an entire day. He came by the house earlier and brought his dad whom he never brought around before, but he wanted him to see his son. All three of them had the same name. I stopped my boyfriend before he left out of the house to tell him that my daughter's dad and grandmother were driving up to come and get her. The reason for me telling him this was because although he and I weren't really on speaking terms, I didn't want him popping up at my house starting trouble. He told me that my daughter's dad couldn't come in the house but the grandmother could. I told him that that was stupid, that it didn't make any sense and every could come in the house. We started arguing of course. I saw that he had a fifth of Hennessy in his back pocket and so I knew this is going to be a long day.

When he left, I began getting my daughter's clothes together, getting the house together and cooking. I was continuously calling his phone because I wanted to make sure he did not come to the house mad. I wanted to let him know that he could come to the house, but I want everything to be peaceful when they come.

Later on, that night, my daughter's grandmother called you let me know they were a couple of hours outside of the city. Right after that phone call, my son's dad came into the house and started arguing and cussing. I thought this night was really weird because he had never done any of that in front of the kids. Even though my daughter was asleep, my son was still up. He began fighting me. I tried to run out the door, but he was ramming my leg in the door. I ran to the kitchen to get a steak Knife just to scare him so I could leave. I was finally able to get outside the house. I ran outside screaming. Nobody is coming outside, no cars are going down the street, and so I stand in front of a house a couple of doors down. He comes outside with a ceramic glass bowl, so I back up. It looks as if he's going to leave because he's walking away from the house. As he's doing that, I ran up the stairs on the porch to run in the house. But before I could, he grabbed me from behind. I turn around, and I stick him with the knife. He was shocked! I was shocked! I ran into the house and locked the door because I thought he was going to kill me. I called the police and told them I'm not opening my door until they get there. They stay on the phone with me until they arrive. The police instructed me to open the door. As I open the door and let them in, I see my son's dad on the top step holding his shoulder with his head down. One cop comes and gets the kids, another one comes and gets me, then handcuffs me. They take me downtown, and all I can think about is the fact that I have a test on Monday, I'm in all of this mess, I have my daughter's dad and grandma on their way. They're going to pull up on a crime scene, and God knows what's going to happen to me in nursing school because you cannot be in any type of trouble in nursing.

So, when I get downtown, I'm sitting in this room, and all I'm thinking about at this point is that I'm so embarrassed that these people are pulling up to a crime scene. I'm not thinking it's serious as it ends up being. 1 Hour. 2 hours. 3 hours. 4 hours and I'm still sitting in this room. I asked the officer if everything was okay? Is my son's dad okay? They told me they didn't know anything and that the detectives would be here soon.... I'm thinking, detectives? Why are we waiting for detectives? Finally, a couple more hours have passed, and the detectives come in. One detective asked if I wanted anything. I told them that my stomach was queasy and that I had been sitting there for a while. The lady says, "we need you to tell us what happened tonight." I began to tell her and then I stopped. I asked her how my son's dad was. She put her hand on my hand and said, honey, he passed away this morning. I lost it right then and there! I couldn't believe this was happening! I looked at my hands and thought, "how did this happen?" I cried I! screamed! I fell out! The first person I thought about was his mom. I thought about his grandma, then I thought about my son not having a dad. I thought about his kids. I just screamed out on the floor uncontrollably. I couldn't get it together because I couldn't understand everything that was happening to me right then and there.

I began to get upset with my son's dad. I said how could you die and I'm the one who has been back and forth in the hospital? How could he die on me after putting me through so much? At the end of the day, that was my son's dad, and although he had his issues, I still loved him. I couldn't believe that I let this get this far. Why didn't I leave? Why didn't I just move out of town? Why did I think by staying it would help anything? How could this tiny knife do this? How could this have happened? I wanted to kill myself! I wanted to die!

I can promise you during that season the only thing that kept me alive was knowing that my kids needed me. I knew I had two kids who did not ask to be in this world. I chose to bring them in this world, and they needed me. I began to get so mad at God because I felt like, why would you talk me into having this baby and you know what's going to happen? The feelings that I had in that season were unbearable. There were some nights when I really believed he would come back to life. I still, for the life of me, could not believe something like this could happen. Not to me! I would ask God out of all of this stuff I went through growing up and all of this stuff my son's dad went through if we we're born just to be set up for devastation, why were we even born?

I don't know that everything is a part of God's plan, but sometimes I feel like the plan has gone wrong. The only thing that either one of us ever wanted was to be loved. In the midst of us trying to find ourselves, and love, we found ourselves and tragedy. Through all of this, I've learned that we cannot heal people. God has to do it! We thought we were two people who had each other's back, and that was all that was needed. But we were two people in pain from past life experiences trying to sustain the best way we knew how.

I am now raising my two children in Atlanta, GA. I am currently finishing my Psychology degree because I am determined to help men and women get their spirit and mind right, in order to live a healthy life and have healthy relationships. I think in order to stop this cycle we have to help heal hearts and minds.

My message to you is this... If you are being abused or are the abuser, I want to urge you to understand that having love for someone doesn't always mean staying. Sometimes, truly loving someone is going far away until real healing can take place. We all have choices to make, and you must, in situations like this, use the mind that God gave you and tell your heart to shhhhh. Remember, that you would not be the only one affected when encountering domestic violence.

SURVIVOR TALK
Goal Setting

Goal setting and proper planning will help you to move forward with your life goals. Mind, body, and soul. If you don't know where you are going, how will you ever know when you get there?

As you begin to take the time to consider your future, writing or journaling each goal will help you to begin to see the vision. Then, once the vision is realized, you will begin to take action to manifest it. Vision takes confidence. Planning requires action.

AFFIRMATION
Today, I will plan my goals and take action so that I reach my next level.

It's time to move forward with your future goals. Career goals, educational goals, spiritual goals, etc… You must do this in spite of the past. In spite of the negative comments or actions of others.

- What are your goals?
- What are your plans for achieving your goals?
- What are the challenges that you feel may interfere with the achievement of your goals?
- How will you celebrate your accomplishment?

Visualize your plan and put it into action – *your life depends on it.*

Chapter Ten

PURPOSELY BROKEN
By LaKeisha Christian

*Pain can either paralyze us or push us.
It's our decision which we choose.
~Lakeisha Christian*

Some people count it a privilege to live in the country. Who wouldn't? The smell of fresh air, birds chirping songs of serenity and the moon and stars in plain sight at night, were not the only perks. Your neighbors were family, roses seemed to always be in bloom (especially at my granny Delias house), and you could sit on the porch and feel peace surrounding you. Of course, now, I appreciate all the country has to offer, but as a child growing up I couldn't wait to grow up, fall in love and be whisked off to my happily ever after.

I grew up in an extremely small town called Gladstone, VA. Population, less than 2,000 people. The roads were gravel, there was one store in walking distance and no stop lights. Our bus ride to school was an entire hour. Yes, you read that right. 60 minutes. 3,600 seconds. That long bus ride and going to church three times a week was not on my list of likes. Now, what did make that list was walking thru the woods with my cousins to pick fruit from the apple tree, collecting honeysuckles (and eating them) and catching lighting bugs.

We didn't have iPhones, Ipads and Mac Books to keep

our undivided attention. Facebook, Twitter, Instagram, and Snapchat? What was that? None of that existed when I was a teenager, including Google. We didn't have conversations with SIRI, we talked to one another. Our days were not consumed with sitting behind a TV playing Xbox all day. We actually made up games to play outside on those long, and hot, summer days. The dirtier we went home, the more fun we had.

The days were especially sweet for me when my Dad would load up me and my siblings in the back of his cream and white 1985 Dodge Ram Van to meet my Mother on her lunch break. That van was his baby, next to me, of course! One of my favorite memories was when he pinned up a blanket between the front and back seats so when my Mom got in she couldn't see us. She got in and questioned why the blanket was there. My dad said, without cracking a smile, "I have trash in the back, I didn't want you seeing it while you eat." That was my cue! BOOM! I tore down the sheet, and we all yelled "Surprise!!"

Birthdays. Holidays. We were always together. Just as a family should be. Of course, there were arguments, but I had grown used to them. Besides, everything was always fine by the next morning.

Life was perfect, until one day I saw my Dad packing his clothes. He threw the bags in the back of his now modified Ram Van and continued to go back and forth into the house, to collect more items I suppose. Finally, I heard the van door close and saw my dad walking towards me. "Kid I have to leave for a while, but I will be back." He picked me up and gave me the tightest hug he had ever given me.

Even now, I don't remember my Mom or Dad telling me

they were getting a divorce, it seems like it just happened. What I do remember is I told myself "It's not your fault." I really didn't know how to feel because I didn't know how to process it. At 8 years old, all I knew was I didn't want my Dad to leave.

I never questioned if my parents loved me, I knew they did. But, when you're a child you don't know how to process "dads no longer here," you just feel that love is no longer near. What I did know was he would no longer be coming home after work, no more family dinners, no more running to Dad when Mom didn't let me have my way, and what I would miss the most, no more calling me by that silly nickname that I secretly loved, Turkey. Even now, I giggle when I say it.

Dad moved out. Mom was working and taking care of home. Life was busy. Their hectic schedules didn't leave much time for hugs, bedtime stories or daily visits. Everyone became comfortable in their way of living and life went on. I quickly learned our new way of life, and I accepted it. But, accepting it didn't mean it was what I deserved.

Of course, then I didn't know that my parents divorcing and lack of affection would lead me on a journey of searching for love, but it did. I am not saying it's their fault. They didn't purposely avoid affection and loving on me. I truly believe they were dealing with all the heartache that comes with divorce. I was lost in the shuffle of two people putting the pieces of their life back together and trying to find who they were without one another.

Years flew by, and it seemed my desire to feel loved grew more and more as I got older. By the time I turned 16, I was sexually active and felt like I could make my own decisions and live like I wanted to. No one could tell me what to do, not even my own parents. I dropped out of school and moved my boyfriend in with me. I became pregnant at 17 and at the age of 18 gave birth to a beautiful baby boy.

I thought I had found what I was like looking for, love. But still, something was missing. I could feel a void inside me that wasn't being filled. A void that made me feel empty and lost. "How could this be? I'm in a relationship with a man who loves me and will do anything for me." Was the haunting question I would ask myself over, and over and over again. I never tried to find the answer. I didn't want to face the answer, so instead, I dug a deep hole within my heart, buried the empty and lost feelings, covered them up and forced myself to forget about them.

Even though my son's father was good to me and the relationship lasted for two years, I knew in my heart that it wasn't my "forever." So, when it was over, it was over. There weren't days of grieving, missing him or crying myself to sleep at night to a New Edition slow song. Nope. None of that! I felt a sense of relief because I could start over fresh. I could do things right and give my son the life he deserved. Shoot, I could give myself the life I deserved!

I fully intended to do just what I said, create a fresh start for me and my baby. I told myself not to get involved with anyone else and to focus on going back to school and raising my son. But those feelings I buried months ago started to surface. The thoughts of needing to be loved became stronger because now I didn't need someone to love just me but me and my newborn son.

As an 18-year-old, I should have been enjoying college, hanging out with friends and sleeping in late. Instead, I worked third shift, changed diapers all day and played peek a boo for me and my son's enjoyment. Although not planned or expected, I never regretted having my son. He brought a joy to me that I had never experienced. But, that joy still was not enough.

Days would drag and nights would be long and lonely. Something was missing, and I just couldn't figure out what. It didn't matter that I just ended a relationship where love didn't fix me, I still thought love was the missing piece to the puzzle. It had to be! Love could come in, sweep me off my feet and rescue me. So, I ignored furthering my education to continue my journey of finding love.

My mission became clear! I had to find someone who would validate, comfort and love me. That one person that would give me a sense of security had to be out there, and it was my goal to find him. The next two years I wondered aimlessly looking for someone that would fulfill and complete me. What I found was a false sense of hope in love, broken promises, disappointment, two more broken relationships and, you guessed it, two more children.

There I was at the age of 20, confused and bewildered. I had already experienced one abusive relationship at 19, no high school diploma, in and out of dead end jobs, three broken relationships and three children depending on me to make a great life for them. I had no answers for my actions because, honestly, I thought it was normal. Why would I think otherwise? It's the only life I ever knew.

Fantasies of my prince charming sweeping me off my feet still existed but now only within the deep parts of my heart. My mind didn't even believe it anymore. Finding someone who would love me and my children seemed like it would be impossible. "Who wants an already made family?" I would often think. All the negativity in my mind combined with my actions was an explosive combination, and it was about to prove itself to be very dangerous. I began to think my life was spiraling out of control but little did I know; the real problems were just about to begin.

The town I now lived in was small, but not as small as the town I grew up in. So, each day on the way home from work I would travel the same route. Every day it was the same routine. Not many turns, not many lights. Straight home to my babies. But this particular Friday things were different. I could see an electric pole had fallen in the distance and traffic had come to a halt. There was nothing I could do, it was too late to turn around and go the only other way there was so I put my car in park and watched the city crew scratch their heads and question the best way to resolve the issue. It was quite entertaining, but the person car next to me obviously didn't think so because he began to blow his horn repeatedly.

I really did not want to look over, but after five minutes of hearing his horn, I decided to just glance and roll my eyes at whoever was being so rude. I was so ready to roll my eyes in disgust but there sitting in the driver's seat was a nice-looking man staring back at me. "You know I was going to blow this horn until you looked, right?" He said with a smile that showed all his pearly whites. I played like I did not hear what he said and nodded my head in a "sure" motion.

My heart was beating out my chest as we sat at the red light exchanging light banter and laughter thru the windows. He was charming, attractive, funny and I could see he was nicely sculpted from the build of his shoulders. I pretended to look past his physical exterior and try to focus on the conversation. After firing off general questions, he asked if I had children. I usually do not tell people I just met personal information but for some reason, "Yes, three wonderful babies." came rolling off my tongue! He didn't flinch and did not look the bit turned off. He proceeded to tell me he did not have any kids of his own but how much he loved them. I quickly added "loves children" to his list of, "said "qualities I was keeping track of in my head. We had become so lost in conversation that we did not hear the horns of drivers warning us that traffic was slowly moving. As we readied ourselves to drive, he reeled me in! He knew exactly what he was doing when he bit his lower lip and said "Keisha, I really enjoyed our conversation. Do you think we could exchange numbers and get to know one another better?" I acted shy but without hesitation blurted my number out. Traffic started moving before he had given me his number so as we were driving he yelled it out. I couldn't make out all the digits with all the noise that was surrounding us, so I failed to get his. I think back now and tell myself how that clearly was a sign! He turned off on his exit, and I continued home. I did not know if I would hear from the stranger I met on Fort Ave. again.

After getting the kids ready for bed, it was my time. Time to unwind and enjoy the remainder of the night before the day started all over in a few hours. I grabbed my favorite blanket, sat in my favorite spot on the couch and turned the television to my favorite channel, The Food Network. Before I could guess what Bobby Flay had in the pot, my phone rang. A local number flashed across my screen. "Could it be Fort Ave guy? Was he really calling so soon? I thought the rule was to call a few days later." I thought to myself.

It was him. I joked with him about clearly not knowing the man made up a rule to wait a few days before calling. The charm continued, "I couldn't wait, I had to talk with you." Oh, how I loved the attention! I sunk down in my seat and was fully captivated by his conversation. We discussed everything from favorite foods, movies, and colors to where we see ourselves in five years. I guess another sign should have been when his answer was "with you." This was the attention I craved. It drew me in, and I loved it.

The conversation continued well into the early morning hours. I felt like I was back in middle school, both of us nodding off and claiming to not be sleep when the other mentioned it. Finally, when I felt I could no longer keep my eyes open, I gave in and said it was time for me to go to bed. We agreed to talk the next day and said our sleepy good byes and hung up. I went to bed excited for what tomorrow would bring.

For the next two weeks, calls came in like clockwork. A call in the morning, one in the afternoon and one in the evening. I always looked forward to the evening call because I knew we would talk for hours about everything, and sometimes about nothing at all. Then one night just before we got off the phone, he asked me to come visit him. I was glad he asked because I was curious as to where he lived and how he lived. Instead of our normal evening call the next day, we decided to meet at his house.

I took one last glance at myself before walking up to the door. Oh, I was cute! I had on a cute outfit, and my makeup was flawless! I felt confident he would think the same, so I made my way to the door and gently knocked on it. As I heard footsteps getting closer, my heart began to beat faster. The door slowly opened, and there stood his MOMMA! She invited me in, and we introduced ourselves to one another. Before the introductions were finished, he came walking in the living room with a huge smile across his face. I forgot all about his mother standing there as I saw his huge brown eyes staring at me. Besides, maybe she was just visiting. "You wanna go to my room?" He asked. "Sure." He opened the basement door and said: "Ladies first." As I started down the steps, I thought to myself "Nope, she's not visiting! He lives with his Mother!"

The longer we talked, the more I did not mind that he lived with his mother. He was a hardworking guy who had made a few bad choices and was now working to save enough money to buy a house. At least, that's what he told me. Who was I to judge him and the bad decisions he made that landed him back at his parents' house? Shoot, that would have been the pot calling the kettle black! I had made quite a few mistakes myself, so I decided to give him a chance. After all, wouldn't he be giving me a chance too? After all the awkwardness had faded, the visit went great! It went so well that we decided to see each other the next day. At my house this time, not his Mothers.

The next few weeks seemed to be a blur to me because we spent every available minute together. He quickly moved in with me and made our home his. You find out a lot when you're living with someone. Like the fact that he did not have a job like he first stated. The car he was driving when I met him? His Mothers. So, there we are. Living in my home, driving my vehicles and spending my money. I went to work every day to take care of home, my babies, and now, a grown man.

Five months into the relationship I noticed the charm he once had was long gone. He would come into the house with a nasty attitude and stay that way for hours. He wouldn't talk to me for the entire evening. It was confusing to me because it seemed like he turned into Dr. Jekyll and Mr. Hyde overnight. I brushed it off and thought maybe he was down because he hadn't found a job yet. I tried encouraging him only to be snapped on "Shut up and get out of my face!" I had never seen him this way before, and I had certainly never heard him talk to me in that manner. I decided to give him some space and let him talk to me when he was ready.

Later that evening after the kids had gone to bed he came into the bedroom. I turned the alarm on my cell phone and, coincidentally, put it down when he walked in. "Hey, babe!" I happily said. All I saw was this huge 6'3 man come charging towards me. I had no time to do anything but to cover my face. He repeatedly slapped me as he yelled "You think I don't know you're cheating on me! I know you have someone else!" My heart was racing as I tried with all my might to cover myself. The last slap was so hard I landed on the floor. I laid there for a minute, still covered, and wondering where he was.

I peeped through my hands and saw him leaning against the wall with his head in his hands crying profusely. I slid myself into the corner of the bed and cried silently so my children could not hear me. A few minutes later I heard his sobbing getting louder. I looked up, and there he stood, looking down at me. I could barely make out what he was saying because he was crying so hard. "I'm sorry! I'm sorry! I don't know why I did that. Please forgive me. Please forgive me!" He repeated that over and over again. I was in shock and didn't say anything. I just listened.

He helped me up and pulled back the covers so I could get in the bed. He laid behind me whispering "I'm so sorry" until he fell asleep. I didn't hear a word he said, my mind was occupied wondering if he had woke the children up. I imagined them lying paralyzed in the bed too scared to move, crying. As soon as I felt his grip released from around my waist, I got up quietly and ran to check on the kids. All three of them were still sound asleep. I sighed a breath of relief and hung my head as I started to walk back towards my room. Why didn't I grab the kids and leave right then? I asked myself the same question.

The next morning, I woke up to the aroma of bacon and eggs. He never cooked breakfast. Why was he this morning? I wasn't hungry, I just wanted to lay in bed and not move. Then I heard my babies giggling. Immediately I jumped up. I washed my face and put on the best fake smile I could find. As I entered the kitchen, he walked towards me and hugged me as tight as he could and whispered, yet again, "I'm sorry, I will never do it again," The sad part? I believed him. Everyone deserves a second chance, right? I hugged him back and said, "I forgive you."

My life became a whirlwind after that day. Everything seemed to be falling apart, including me. We were now in search of a new home because of an eviction due to "suspicious activity" happening in our home. The abuse became worse, and the apologies grew in numbers. My confidence and self-esteem were nonexistent. I felt worthless, undeserving and guilty. Was I too social like he said? Was I really flirting and did not know it? I began to believe I was the cause of the black eyes, broken bones, bruises and broken promises of "never doing it again."

After moving into our new home, that was too small and isolated from neighbors, I decided it was time to put the kids in daycare. The next day I left early to visit a few that I had scribbled down on paper. Noah's Ark was a beautiful big daycare full of vibrant kids who were not only being prepared for Kindergarten but were also taught Gods Word. I loved it and was ready to place all three in their care. I filled out the application and was approved! There was only one problem, they only had space for one child. Since my oldest was going to kindergarten the following year, I thought he was the best fit. He was enrolled. One down. Two to go.

As I was walking out the door, the director of the daycare ran to me and handed me a piece of paper. "We have a great woman who just opened a home daycare, I think your kids will love it there!" She boasted of her former employee's qualifications and told me she had already called and told her we were on the way. I thanked her and told her we would go straight there.

It was only five minutes from where we were so we quickly pulled up. As I surveyed her home and neighborhood, a woman appeared at the door with a smile big as Texas. I was so jealous of her straight white teeth! She welcomed us into her home and gave us the tour of "Little Lambs." Which didn't take long at all because the house was small. Cozy but small. The children immediately connected with her and, to my surprise, so did I. I'm sure she saw me looking around confused as to why there was only one child in her daycare and begin to explain to me she had just opened a month ago. She interacted with the kids while we continued talking about possible enrollment. Although I had reservations, something told me to this was the daycare for my two.

I went home with a sense of accomplishment and peace. The kids were all enrolled in school, which meant I could go to work and know they were safe. I did not expect him to be home as he said he had errands to run, but there he sat in silence in the living room. I knew he had conjured something up in his mind as to where I was. He asked me to take the kids to their room and shut their door. By this time, I knew what was about to happen, I just didn't know why. But did I ever?

I put the kids all in one room, cut the television on and up and shut the door. He met me in the kitchen. I leaned against the counter and waited for him to speak. I knew not to talk first. "Where have you been?" I told him everywhere I went, in detail. "That is a lie!" he yelled. I stayed quiet. Why defend myself if I would only be hit anyway? Besides, I was tired of defending the truth. He grabbed my hand, placed my fingers in the silverware drawer and slammed it as hard as he could. He then picked me up and slammed me on the hard kitchen floor and begin to kick me. The pain that surged through my body was excruciating, but my children were just down the hall and would hear if I screamed. Being abused for almost two years now taught me many lessons. Like, how to scream with my mouth shut, so that's what I did. I took all the pain I was feeling and screamed without saying a word.

I woke up the next day and had to drag myself out of bed. My body was sore from being kicked on a hard, cold floor, four of my fingers felt as if they were broken and now bruises were visible on my legs and arms. I couldn't let that stop me,

I never did. It was summer, and it seemed the sun was shining extra bright that day, but I still chose to put on pants and a long sleeve shirt. When you're in an abusive relationship, you master the techniques of "covering," makeup and long clothing become your best friend. We think the second coat of foundation and layers of clothing help to hide the abuse. The truth is, it doesn't. It illuminates it.

When we arrived at Little Lambs Daycare, I put on my sunshades and slowly got out of the vehicle. I walked as normal as I could, hurting with each step I took. Pam, the day care owner, met us at the door "Come on in guys!" "Could this woman really be this perky every day?" I thought to myself as we all went inside. I lingered around just for a little while to make sure the kids were settling in fine. When I saw they were ok, I turned to leave, but not before Pam says, "You know God loves you, right?" Why was this woman that I didn't even know telling me God loved me? I shook my head yes, smiled and walked to my car.

Every morning before I left the daycare Pam would give me a little nugget to take with me. I never told her, but I looked forward to hearing them each day. Especially if I had a rough night. They gave me hope and motivation. She never questioned me although I believe she knew. She had to because at times the bruises could not be hidden. Especially the one on my heart.

Pam and I quickly become best friends. Bringing the kids to daycare and picking them up made me feel alive. Normal. We would talk and laugh about any and everything. Everything but the abuse. I didn't bring it up, and she didn't ask. I just wanted to be free, if just for an hour, and she allowed me to be.

Months went by, but the abuse never stopped. It did, however, worsen. Although I was sure she knew, my secret was about to be exposed. I didn't have to tell her what was going on and she no longer had to guess because she was about to witness the abuse first hand. I thought I would feel ashamed that it was finally being uncovered but I wasn't. I was relieved. I wanted someone, besides his friends, to know.

It was always the same old tired accusations being brought against me. "I know you are with someone else!" I was so over it. As he walked in the bedroom, I grabbed my keys and ran out the door. Quickly hopped in my car, locked the doors and turned the key. I saw him sprint out behind me. I hated breaking the law, but this day I was speeding trying to get to Pam's house as was right behind me. I finally pulled up, jumped out and ran in the house. I'm sure the slamming of the door startled her because she immediately ran into the living room. "What's going on?" she said in a calm but firm voice. I pointed to the door as he rushed in. There stood this 150 lb., 5 foot 6 woman between me and this 240 lb., 6 foot 2 gorilla. I could feel his rage ricocheting from his body to mines, and I saw beads of sweat exuding through his pores. His eyes seemed to pierce my soul, and he never looked away.

"You have to leave this house NOW!" Pam said looking right into his hateful eyes. She never backed down, never looked away. "Leave, NOW!" He clenched both fists tightly, bit his bottom lip (how could I ever think that was attractive!) and started to breathe faster and louder. I braced myself for impact as I thought he was about to go right through Pam to get to me. Instead, he did something I had never seen him do, slowly back away and then leave.

In that moment, the cute "little nuggets" Pam used to dispense went right out the window. It was time for hardcore tough love. Pam sat down next to me, looked me right in the eyes and told me without hesitation "You need to leave him before he kills you!" I didn't say anything, what could I say? She was right. The thought had been on my mind for quite some time. I looked up to heaven, closed my eyes and silently asked God to send me a quick, but safe, exit plan.

Later that night, I received a phone call from him begging me to come home. He had seen the errors of his ways, again, and was ready to seek professional help for his abusive ways. Against my better judgment and Pam's warning, I went home. I cannot believe I went home just hours after this man had turned into The Incredible Hulk! But, this was the first time he mentioned seeking real help. I thought, just maybe, this time he was telling the truth.

He wasn't. I was a fool to believe him again! Was I so desperate that I had to be with someone who burned me with cigarettes and left scars all over my body? No. I wasn't desperate, I was hopeless. He had embedded in my mind that no one else would want a ready-made family. He made me feel I was useless and not worthy of an abuse free love. I felt I had no other options, so I stayed.

He loved drinking gin. I hated when he did. One particular night he came home so intoxicated that I wondered how he made it. I heard him struggling to get the key in the door. I didn't go help as I wanted to act sleep, hoping he would just pass out and not disturb me. Finally, the door swung open and I heard him plop down on the sofa. "Hopefully he will stay there until morning" I remember thinking to myself. I forced myself to stay woke so I could hear his every move. Minutes later he started walking down the hall, leaning up against the wall so he would not fall. He undressed and got into the bed.

He pressed his body against mines and wrapped his arm around my waist. The odor was so pungent it made my stomach turn. He started to caress my back, then my thighs. His heavy touch was revolting, and it made me feel filthy. He began to kiss my shoulders while turning me over at the same time. Tears begin to fall down my cheeks as he tried to take my shirt off. Without even thinking I heard myself say "No. Stop." He brushed off what I said and continued tugging at my clothes.

I could not take the repulsive feeling any longer. I jumped up so fast I knocked the lamp off the table. It wasn't loud, but it was loud enough to wake my oldest son. "Mommy?" he quietly said. I ran into his room, picked him up and patted his back until he went back to sleep. I was comfortable in my son's room because my abuser never acted out directly in front of them before. But, tonight was different. I had smelled his breath before he said one word. I knew he was standing in the doorway.

"Why don't you want to have sex with me? Because you had sex with your boyfriend today? I know you're sleeping with someone else" he said slurring every other word. He continued to hurl insult after insult at me. I had heard it all before, so it didn't affect me. I was deaf to it.

I quickly laid my son down because I knew he was about to attack. I stood up hoping he would follow me back into our bedroom. When I got close to him, he pushed me down with all his might. I landed on my son's bed, inches from him. He made his way over to me and placed his left hand around my neck. His hand grew tighter and tighter around my neck as I fought to breathe. I could feel my breathing slowing down. Suddenly I heard another voice gasping for air. With the little bit of strength, I had, I felt for his right hand. There it was around my five-year-old son's fragile neck. My body went limp, and in that moment, I completely gave up. "If you're going to take me, TAKE ME! But do not take my son, God!" I cried out in my head.

What happened next surprised me. Right when I cried out, he immediately released us both and staggered back in the bedroom. I coughed uncontrollably as I picked my son up. He was still asleep and breathing! I held him close to me as tears were streaming down my face. I knew what I had to do and I could not wait any longer. If I did, I knew what my fate would be. God had thrown me a life raft, and it was time to use it.

I heard no movement. I laid my son down and quietly tiptoed to the door way to see where he was. Finally, he had passed out. There he lay, naked and helpless. Everything he had ever done to me flashed before my eyes. All the pain he had ever caused me started to speak, and for once, I wasn't scared. He beat a helpless girl, me, for 2 years, and there he lay in the same position. I felt empowered in a way. I sat in the doorway and questioned how I could take his life and get away with it.

After what seemed like an eternity I finally came to my senses, which wasn't much at the time. I knew I needed to go before he woke up or before I ended up in handcuffs. I grabbed my purse, picked up one baby in each arm and woke my oldest up to walk. I secured them in the truck and then got in myself. I locked the door, turned on the ignition and took a long look at the home we would not be returning back to.

Pam didn't hesitate to open the door. She grabbed one of the babies and helped us inside. She handed me an extra blanket and tucked them in the warm bed that we would share for the night. Before heading back to her room, Pam turns and looks at me and says "I'm glad you're here. Goodnight!" My heart felt so much gratefulness that God chose to place her in my life, and I couldn't help but to thank God. Where else would we have gone if not there?

The very next day Pam and my friend Amber (another domestic violence survivor) wasted no time to get me and my children's things. We went to my home when he wasn't there and loaded everything that was mine, which was everything, in our cars. We drove down the highway with an entire apartment in three different vehicles. Furniture and all. I had no place to live, so we put everything in storage. The next few days were filled with ideas on what me and the children could do to get a stable home. None of which were immediate. Although Pam had a business she was running out of her home she still offered us to stay there as long as we needed.

Later that evening I received a phone call where he was threatening suicide. He begged me to come back and made more promises to seek mental attention. This time there was no thinking about it. I. Was. Done. I had made it out alive, and there was no way I was going back to a life of abuse. I spoke to him and told him we were not coming back but that he should pursue seeking help. Without warning, I hung up the phone. I knew God heard my prayer because he never bothered us again.

We stayed with Pam for a week or so, but Amber insisted me and the kids come stay with her. That means it would be seven people in her two-bedroom apartment. That didn't matter to her, she just wanted to help. Since she would not take no for an answer, I graciously accepted her offer. We gathered our clothes and went to her house to settle in. Yes, it was cramped, but we were safe.

After going through such a terrible ordeal, I was left picking up pieces and trying to fit them back together again. He had controlled every area of my life, and now that he wasn't around, I had no idea what to do. My entire life was in shambles. I had nothing. He had broken my heart and my spirit. I would look in the mirror only to hate the image that was looking back at me. I hated him, but I hated myself more. I hated him for abusing me, and I hated myself for allowing him. I hated him for degrading me, and I hated myself for believing it.

After months of pity parties, breakdowns, losing weight and questioning God, it was time to make some hard decisions. Live like a victim or become a survivor? Be bitter or be better? Live a life of despair or a life of happiness? It didn't take long for me to decide I wanted to live and I wanted to live an abundant life full of joy, happiness, and peace. It was time to transition my entire life, and it started with God.

I was so thankful to have a support system who stood by my side and helped me when the days were rough. Thankful that they guided me in the right direction by giving me the word of God and not the word of "Pam or Amber." I could never say thank you enough for all they did for me, but all the glory goes to God! It was He who placed them in my path

and He (once I surrendered) who changed my entire life.
Was it difficult for me to surrender my life to Christ? YES!
You better believe it! Relinquishing all control to God was
hard! "I just escaped a domestic violence relationship where
I was a puppet! I'm just now regaining control of my life, and
you want me to give it away again, God?" Was my real
thought! Let's be real! I wasn't the one. You were not going to
trick me again! But then, after much prayer and reading the
word of God, I realized that surrendering my life to Christ
meant that His plans for me would always be in my best
interest.

I couldn't heal myself! I would have only made a bigger
mess of things! For years I fed only that which was negative.
It was time to start feeding the positive. I had to ALLOW God
that control to give me complete open-heart surgery. I
opened my bible every day and read how much God loved
me, His goodness towards me and who I was created to be in
Him. At times, it was uncomfortable and unbelievable
because I had years of insults, criticism, and hatred instilled
in my mind. But, I continued to pray, and I continued to
read. The more food I ate (The Word of God), the more I
would regurgitate the negative.

His word really did become a lamp for my feet and a
light on my path (Psalm: 105). He was all I had in the
midnight hour when I was alone. My flesh was lonely and
would urge me to get into another relationship, but my spirit
would cry out "NO! Trust God." The enemy tried all he could
to convince me that I should go back! But, how many of you
know that God always has an exit strategy? See, I
remembered how James 4:7 told me to "Resist the devil, and
he will flee from you," and that's exactly what I did in those

moments of struggle! I clinched the word close to my heart and watched the enemy tuck his tail and run!

As I look back on everything, I went through I see God was always there. When the pain was unbearable, He gave me the strength to keep going. When I was too weak to walk, He carried me. When I would turn over and cry in the middle of the night, He would wipe away my tears and soothe my aching heart. When I had no one, He placed people in my path to encourage and support me, and when I thought I was going to die, He kept back the hand of death and saved me.

I continue to affirm myself daily because let's face it, there is an adversary who wants to steal, kill and destroy (John 10:10) who we are destined to be. I constantly remind myself of the God I serve and how much He loves me. The Lord is my strength and shield (Psalm 28:7). His love covered me and filled every empty space and void that was in my life then, and still does today. He shattered the walls I had built around my heart to keep anyone out and taught me how to trust someone to love me and how to love them back, all through His love for me. He did the miraculous and healed not only the visible scars but also the scars on my heart. No man or woman could ever do that for me or for you! The true love we seek is in the Father! It is He who will love us unconditionally.

You see, the pain I endured was never meant to kill me. It was purpose. Purpose for such a time as this to tell my story and help all who are going, or have gone, through the same. I was purposely broken because He knew that the pain I carried secretly for years would push me to yield my life to Him and forever give His name the glory.

If you ever have a question as to what love is, here's the

best definition I have ever found.

Love is patient, love is kind. It does not envy, it does not boast, it is not proud. It does not dishonor others, it is not self- seeking, it is not easily angered, it keeps no record of wrongs. Love does not delight in evil but rejoices with the truth. It always protects, always trust, always hopes always perseveres. 1 Corinthians 4 :7

Know The Cycle

It never failed, after I would get choked, punched, slapped, kicked, burned or verbally attacked, my abuser would then use the same cycle below to make me believe that he would change and that the abuse wouldn't happen again. That's not true, in fact, the cycle only repeats itself. Time and time and time again. If you are a victim, know that the cycle of abuse is just what Webster defines it is: Any complete round or series of occurrences that repeats or is repeated. Break the cycle.

Knowledge is the key to a better understanding. Knowing the signs and cycle of abuse can save lives. If you are currently in a domestic violent relationship, struggling with the mental anguish of leaving one, you can be set free, healed and live a life of abundance! It starts with YOU! You have to decide which path to take, life or death. The day you decide that you want to live is the day your life of freedom will begin! God wants to give you a crown of beauty for ashes, oil of joy instead of mourning and a garment of praise for the spirit of heaviness! (Isaiah 61:3) IF YOU ALLOW HIM.

Continue praying and reading the word of God. Let every word He says about you sink deep into your soul and fill the very essence of who you are. Let the love He freely gives comfort you in times of sorrow, as well as in times of joy. Allow Him to place the right people around you that will love you beyond your faults! Everyone needs a "Pam" in their life, but if you don't have one, you can borrow mines anytime you need her. She will always be right here to push you to your greatness!

"My friend, you are so brave and have so much courage inside you! I am so proud of you for making the right decision to leave, you're protecting yourself and your children. Don't you ever regret making the right decision. You are setting an example for your children to never tolerate abuse by anyone's hands. I thank God for the person He has made you to be. Remember, God loves you and He will never leave you!

Congratulations on your road to love, peace and happiness."

Your friend,
Pamela Fisher

SURVIVOR TALK
Signs that you may be in an abusive relationship

- Monitors what you are doing all of the time.
- Unfairly accuses you of cheating or being unfaithful
- Prevents you from talking to or seeing friends or family
- Tries to prevent or discourage you from going to work or school
- Gets very angry due to drug or alcohol use.
- Controls how you spend your money
- Decides things for you that you should be allowed to decide (like what to wear or eat)
- Humiliates you in front of others
- Destroys your property or things that you care about
- Threatens to hurt you, the children, or pets
- Hurts you (by hitting, beating, pushing, shoving, punching, slapping, kicking, or biting)
- Uses (or threatens to use) a weapon against you
- Forces you to have sex against your will
- Blames you for their violent outbursts
- Threatens to harm himself or herself when upset with you
- Says things like, "If I can't have you then no one can."

If you think someone is abusing you, get help.

When God said "My grace is sufficient for you," He promises us the grace to survive whatever pain, suffering or trials we are experiencing. He does not promise to take the pain away, but the strength to survive it.

~Wounds to Wisdom

Chapter Eleven

UNBREAKABLE
A Life Worth Fighting For
By Pamela Morgan

I'm no longer a slave to fear. I am a child of God.

It was fall 1995; I was a young, naïve immigrant from the Philippines when I met him. I was 18 years old, a senior in high school when I walked into my first day working for a retail-clothing store when he asked me out, and I accepted. He was cute and charming. He was older which added to the appeal. He said he was a college student, yet obviously very rebellious.

He encouraged me to do what felt good and fun regardless of consequence. My mother demanded I never see him again, but I was drawn. I attended private Catholic schools all my life. I was to be faithful, pure and obedient. He convinced me it was the "adult thing to make my own choices" since I was 18 and as such my mother cannot tell me what to do anymore. Disobeying the rules for a change was fun. He empowered me to go out and do what I thought was fun at the time and it felt good for once to be in control.

A few months into dating, I found out he was on probation for aggravated assault. He said it was because he plead guilty to avoid a trial. He had stabbed his ex-girlfriend's father when he walked in on him beating her. In a few weeks, he would be in jail for violating that probation.

I contemplated breaking up with him then. I really can't

explain why I didn't. I'm loyal, I guess.

While he was in jail, he would call me and drill me on what I did all day and whom I spent those days with. If it were any of my male friends, he freaked out and accused me of cheating. A good girlfriend would not cheat especially when their boyfriends are in jail. I am a special kind of a whore. When I would hang up on him, he would call back and say he's sorry it's just that he loved me so much and didn't want to lose me because another guy might charm me. Slowly, I started to pull away from my friends.

He was released July 1996. Within a month, I was pregnant. That was only just a couple months after I graduated high school. I had plans to go to college, which was now "on hold." The pregnancy was not planned for me, but I suspect it was for him. Yet he accused me of cheating, and the baby was not his. I was trapped and very scared. I begged him to believe me, on my hands and knees that I hadn't been with anyone ever; not before I met him, not while I was with him, not even once had I been with another man.

Being pregnant with his child made me feel trapped. How could I leave him now? He wanted me to marry him, but I said no. It didn't feel right to marry him. I moved in with him though, in his mother's basement. He didn't have a full-time job, but I had my part-time job working as a cashier at retail store. While I worked, he spent his day running around northern New Jersey buying or stealing drugs. He didn't hide it then, his drug use, though I wasn't too sure what drugs he was using. Whatever it was, he smoked it through a pipe, and it wasn't weed.

His jealousy would progress, even as my belly grew

bigger. He would walk in the store while I worked to spy on me and watch every time another guy spoke to me. He watched every time I walked to the back area to use the ladies' room. I used it a lot since I was pregnant. He would then question me about all of these encounters as soon as he picked me up. He swore I was going to the back to have quickies with the guys that I spoke to. He would apologize every time and say he wouldn't get so jealous if I just stopped flirting with people. He considers conversations as flirting. I would slowly learn to walk with my head down to avoid looking towards any man to help him not think I was trying to flirt.

At around 6 or 7 months pregnant, I decided I wanted out; this was not what I thought it would be. I had imagined a much happier time expecting a baby, not misery and torment on a daily basis. I felt like a prisoner. He begged me to come back and that he will stop as soon as the baby is born. He just needed to get high as much as possible now to get all that partying desires out before the baby was born. I was young and dumb, and I fell for it.

The baby was born, and he didn't stop. He just started hiding it and lying about it. He would take off leaving Samantha and me alone for days and then come back as if he just went to work for the day. He would come home and interrogate me on what I did while he was gone. He would accuse me of having another man at the house. I didn't even have a car to go anywhere because he had it.

When Sam was four months old, he applied for a job to become a superintendent of an apartment complex so we could have a place to live free. We packed up and moved. He worked some, quoted the owner for supplies needed for purchase. His brother would come and pick him up to get the checks from the owner, and they would spend it on themselves to get high for days. Again, he would come back home screaming at me that I had another man in his home while he was gone. It was a combination of his jealous, controlling rage and his way for me not to confront him for spending all ours and the property owner's money on drugs.

In six months, he was fired, and we were evicted. I guess we were lucky the property owner had not filed criminal charges with theft of goods and services.

He would apply at another apartment complex for another superintendent job and get it. We move again, but this time, he was fired in four months. It was at this point that I talked to my mother for help. I need to go to college and get some kind of career. I obviously can't rely on him to provide for his child. I had planned to enroll in the fall semester 1998.

However, I got pregnant again. Baby #2 would be due November 1998. Fall semester is out, but I was determined. I enrolled for the winter semester. Grace was born November 5th, I was in school by January 3rd, 1999. We moved in at my mom's house so she could help me with the girls while I attended class. I knew the only way I could do this is with the help of my mother. She has been a wonderful blessing even through her disappointments.

One night mid-January 1999, I receive a phone call from the police station. He had just been arrested for multiple charges including check fraud, assault on a police officer, and destruction of public and private property when he led the cops on a high-speed chase through Linden and Roselle Park areas and into a golf course. He had been bingeing on crack cocaine for days and was hoping to get cash by buying cartons of cigarettes using old checks and reselling them for half the price. He had bounced checks at this store before so they denied his purchase, which led to an altercation.

I can't remember all the charges against him, but it had about $35,000 bail. His mother bonded her house, bailed him out, and hired an attorney for him. We went to court for the initial hearing and watched the prosecutor hand his attorney his discovery file. It was approximately 6 inches thick. Documents contained some information about all his charges plus his prior criminal record. His past record alone was maybe 4 inches thick.

His attorney arranged for him to go to a long-term drug rehabilitation facility if he plead guilty, using his addiction as an excuse for his criminal behavior. He accepted but demanded I marry him before he left, or he would run to Mexico and the kids will never see their father again. I hesitated but agreed, for the girls' sake. I believed they needed their father and this was the only chance left for him to straighten out.

We got married on my birthday, 1999. While he was at the rehab, I attended school. Still, he consistently attempted to control every action I made. He wanted to know everything I did, every person in my class, who sat next to me and who I spoke with.

He spent about a year in the rehabilitation house before he completed the judge's requirements and was released on probation. He came home, started working and bought himself a safe. Every penny he made went straight into the safe. I wasn't allowed to just take any money out without his permission. One day Samantha outgrew the one and only pair of sandals she owned, and I told him I needed $20 to buy her new ones. He said 'no' and came home with a couple of hand-me-down sandals from his niece. Why spend any money when he has a niece, he says. Meanwhile, he comes home wearing a nice heavy gold chain necklace. His reward for himself for staying sober for so long.

Eventually, he would relapse and start following me to school. He would sit in the parking lot all day long with the girls waiting for me to come out during breaks. He would make me identify who was who, and I'd have to convince him that I was not having an affair with all the guys in my class. Eventually, my entire class knew he was crazy, and I was beyond humiliated. He would insist on putting giant hickies on my neck before I go to class; it was his way of "marking his territory" and make sure all these guys knew to stay away from me.

Miraculously, I graduated technical school, received my diploma in Web Development and Business Programming with honors, and got a job offer with a Fortune 500 insurance company. The job offer required a 3-month training with eight other new hires. I was one of only two females. Again, he would question everything I did while in class and demanded I call home every hour so he can check the phone number I called from and make sure I was where I said I was. It was impossible to call every hour because I was in classes. He wasn't pleased and of course, "I'm the whore that sleeps with everyone while he stayed home to raise the kids." A few months later, I got pregnant with our 3rd child, a boy this time. He would insist on naming him his junior.

I was a great developer and impressed my superiors. I was rated high on my annual reviews and received huge pay raises and bonuses I never could have imagined. In 4 years, I would double my salary. All the while, he would torment and terrorize me and accuse me of having affairs with all the men that work in my building.

When I got home, he would check my body and clothing including my underwear for signs I had sex that day with someone else. Every day he would point at the birthmark on my neck and claim it was a hickey. I would remind him I had that mark all my life, yet he would call me a lying whore because he would be convinced that mark was never there before.

He would question everything I wore to work every day. He would point out my underwear was "too sexy" one day so I would wear one of my really old ones, but he would scream they were too old and torn I must be wearing them so my boyfriend could easily rip them off me. He would get so upset if I shaved my legs or even bothered showering at all. Anything I did he suspected because I was going to have some wild hot sex with another man while I was at work. I didn't own a skirt or dress because they were "easy access."

I would spend plenty of sleepless nights fighting with him that I had not had any affairs at all. I would go to work restless. He would ring my phone at work numerous times a day making sure I'm at my desk. If I had a meeting, I had to call him, and he would scream I'm a liar, and I'm just going to have sex with my lover. I would unplug my phone before each meeting so it wouldn't ring and disrupt anyone working around me while I was away.

If I had to use the restroom, I had to call him and let him know, so he didn't freak out if I didn't answer my phone. Then he would time how long I was in the bathroom. Most of the time I took "too long" which meant I must have had a "quickie with my boyfriend."

In the summer of 2004, I left work early to get a protective order against him and have him removed from my home. That night I woke up in the middle of the night hearing some noise outside my townhome and my home phone line dead. I looked out the window and saw him climbing through the basement window. I ran down the stairs to lock and block the basement door, but I was too late. I ran back upstairs where he caught on to me in the hallway. That night was the worst physical altercation he and I had. I tried screaming, but he held my throat down and tried to put a pillow on my face. I fought him as hard as I could. I remember him punching me in the stomach numerous times. I saw Sam and Grace crying so hard, Sam with her arms and hands around her little sister protecting her and shielding her from seeing their parents fight brutally on the floor.

I got away from him and ran down the stairs, practically naked, as my clothes had been torn. I got out of the house and pounded on my neighbor's door for help. He ran on foot into the woods as my neighbor called 9-1-1. Cops searched for him for a couple of hours until eventually, they found him. They also found a knife in the upstairs hallway just outside my bedroom.

The next day, my body was sore. I went into the emergency room, and the doctor says my entire back was very tender. Sure enough, two days later, over 50% of my body was black and blue; from my shoulders, arms, down my back and my entire right leg.

Again, he plead guilty and went into drug rehab for

treatment... the drugs made him do it again. I can't really explain other than I fell for his promises, but once he

completed the program, I accepted him back. He would stay sober for a few months then relapse again, but all the while, his jealousy never stopped.

Some mornings he would leave while I was getting dressed for work to keep me from leaving. I called out of work a lot. If I made it into work, I was severely late. I made up plenty of excuses. Eventually, I had to have a private conversation with my manager about what was going on in my life. She helped me as much as she could, but eventually, she had to let me go because I was more of a risk and liability than an asset.

One day, I was mentally and emotionally worn out. He spent the morning calling me at work repeatedly screaming and accusing me of not being at work and being with my phantom lover. I would hang up the phone, and he would call again. He threatened I would never see my children again... He threatened with unimaginable things to me and my children. He rang my phone endlessly that my colleagues pulled my office phone off the wall.

I found an empty office and just crawled underneath the desk. I laid there on the floor, underneath the desk in that dark office crying so hard, I was at my lowest point and felt so helpless. I remember the feeling that I was severely drowning and I can't see where the surface was to take a breath. I wanted to just take my kids, hold them tight and disappear somewhere with them where he couldn't find us, but he has them, and I just didn't know what to do anymore.

I found a phone and called Bev, the other female in my training class when I first started working there. I had confided in her before. I asked her to please tell our manager I needed to go home. She heard something in my voice and went to look for me. Once she found me, she told me she would take me home and told our manager. What I didn't know at that time was Bev had sensed I could be thinking suicide. I never could understand how she knew. I never told anyone I thought of suicide. Not one soul knew how I realized just a couple months before that between my life and accident insurance my children would get almost half a million dollars. No one knew that every day I drove home through I-78 and passed an 18-wheeler, I had thought if I could just swerve my tiny little car, slightly that truck would instantly kill me and it would look like an accident rather than suicide.

However, Bev knew and rather than take me home, she took me to the nearest hospital and told me to tell them what has been going on or she would. I broke down and told them I wanted to kill myself. I was admitted quickly and put into an observation room. Bev was allowed to stay while I was in observation, and she stayed almost all day and into the early evening.

Meanwhile, he was wondering where I was, determined I had run off with my lover. I had called my mother-in-law and asked her to please keep an eye out on my kids while I got some help for myself. I told her where I was, but asked, please do not tell my mother.

Two days in the hospital mental health ward, I receive a message that Lisa, one of my sister-in-law's, had called and asked if I could call her back. She had taken custody of my children away from him because he went to their house screaming about some men in black following him and trying to kill him. She came to see me at the hospital the next day, with my mom as she took the kids from her.

While I was in the hospital, I saw counselors and therapists and was prescribed anti-depressants and anti-anxiety pills. However, the one thing they all said was the meds are only temporary just to keep my mind and emotions at bay while I figure out my permanent solution. I knew what that permanent solution was; I just didn't know how to achieve it yet. They even brought in a counselor who was a recovering addict and had a story of drug abuse so severe you wondered how he was still alive. I spoke to him and his only advice is to "stay away from him. He's a sociopath!" I spent eight days in the hospital.

The months leading after my brief hospital stay did not improve my situation. Frankly, it may have made things worst. The anti-depressants allowed me to keep a stable level head while he caused havoc around me. I knew I had to take my kids and leave, but I also knew I had to plan this thoroughly for our safety. It was hard because he always took one kid with him, usually my son, whenever he left. I guess he knew I would be leaving any day now.

The career that I had excelled on has been flushed down the toilet. However, the loss of my job was probably a blessing in disguise. I was able to focus on how to get out.

In August 2006, I received one of my unemployment checks. Suddenly he wanted money, I can't remember what he claimed to need it for, but knowing him, I could tell he wanted to get high. I clenched onto my purse for my life all night. Because I refused to give him any money, he ran out the door, screaming and cussing. He would leave, after stealing my bank card, then come back so high he was neurotic insane. I had laid on the couch to sleep. He would come in saying he was just outside and he watched my boyfriend leave. He would try to grab me and stick his hands into my pants to check if I had just had sex. He would smell me and scream that I smell like a whore who just had sex. I told him to leave, or I would call the cops. He left, and I called his sister and told her what he has been doing to me.

His sister would come and pick the kids and me up to go to her house for refuge in the morning. My dear friend Lily, who lived over an hour away, decided she was coming to visit for the day rather than go to work. He would drive by his sister's house screaming that his sister is allowing me to have sex with my lover at her house. Lily would walk down and calm his down. He would leave and come back again later on. His sister's husband would try to calm him down but ended up punching him in the face.

Police came but could not issue him any criminal citation because "he hasn't done anything illegal." If they did, they would have to arrest my sister-in-Law's husband for assault. They did file a complaint for me, and I was granted a protection from abuse order against him again; the third one I had received since I married him 7 years prior.

It wasn't easy, but this time I knew there was no taking him back. He thought this would just be another one of those times he just needed to go to rehab and we will be back again. I didn't care at this point. I was done. I knew I had to be very careful. Every time I walked out the door, I looked down the street to make sure there were no suspicious vehicles or persons watching my home. I looked in my rearview mirror more often than not making sure he was not following me. My neighbor did see him driving by the house at least once.

My mother helped me pay my rent. I couldn't file for divorce right away because I was in debt and jobless. I had applied numerous companies for jobs and didn't get an offer. By late October, my unemployment was set to run out, so I

went to a temporary agency for any job. That same day I was offered a temporary job at a bakery plant.

My first day was November 9, 2006. My office was in the maintenance department where I met the engineer whose office was next to mine. He would introduce himself as Marc and said if I ever needed anything do not hesitate to ask. It was not love at first sight. In fact, I wore baggy sweatshirts and a baseball cap every day for work. I didn't want to be noticed. I carried shame on my shoulders.

Eventually, our friendship turned into something else. It was definitely scary, and definitely, the last thing I thought I needed. How would a man want to be involved with someone like me with all the drama in my life? Why would a decent man want to date a 29-year-old mother of three? Nevertheless, he was different. There was something very genuine with him. He was truly kind and loving. The true test was when he met my kids. My girls immediately fell-in-love with him. He felt very safe and secure. My girls didn't want to leave his side. It was then I knew I needed to let go and let things happen. God has protected me all this time, I had no doubt He is still protecting us and paving a path.

Marc would become my constant support and my best friend. He would encourage me to find my identity and grow into the woman I was supposed to be since I was suppressed from becoming her for the last few years. I realized, with Marc, I didn't need to call him all the time and tell him every step I take and make sure he was okay with it. I realized I was finally free.

On April 10, 2009, Marc would propose in front of my kids and on July 10, 2010, he and I would become husband and wife.

I learned so much about abuse and the telltale signs. How they charm you and groom you, then they entrap you by alienating you from everyone who loves you. Abuse is about control, and it doesn't have to be physical. Emotional bruises take longer to heal. 11 years away from him and relocating south, I still look over my shoulders from time-to-time. I had recently filed another restraining order due to his continued constant harassment, this time the judge granted me a lifetime protection order.

Part of my purpose now is to add my voice to the many other survivors and let the world know domestic violence happens more often than anyone believes. I am only one voice, but it will serve to raise awareness for another who may not believe they are living in an abusive relationship.

SURVIVOR TALK
The Power of Loving Yourself

Loving yourself is very key to your happiness and emotional well-being. It is a fact that many people are not even aware of. Love is a powerful force in our lives and can be used to remedy many heartaches and pain. It gives us clarity of mind and motivation to be a better person. It helps us achieve greater things for ourselves—mind, body, and spirit.

Love Yourself!

7 Steps to Begin Loving Yourself

1. Get rid of negative influences
2. Take the time to do things that bring you joy
3. Step out of your comfort zone
4. Pray/meditate
5. Stop criticizing yourself
6. Be gentle, kind, and patient with yourself
7. Forgive yourself

From every wound there is a scar, and every scar tells a story.
A story that is your testimony.
~Wounds to Wisdom

Chapter Twelve

SLEEPING WITH THE ENEMY
By Tamiko Lowry-Pugh

God is not punishing you, He's preparing you.
~Tamiko Lowry Pugh

I remember watching the hit movie "Sleeping with the Enemy" starring the beautiful Julia Roberts back in 1991. In the movie, a young woman found herself having to fake her own death in order to escape her abusive husband. The husband was emotionally, mentally, and physically abusive. He also had an obsession with organizing his cupboards, and hand towels. He wanted everything to be perfect. Including his wife. I thought to myself; this would never happen to me. Fast forward 13 years later. I found myself in a very similar situation.

A few of my coworkers that were excitingly successful at finding great dates on a new Online Dating website insisted that I should try it out. They boasted about dates with nice men that led to great relationships; and ultimately to marriage. So, I decided to give it a try. So, I set up my Dating Profile Page. Then, about an hour later I received my first message from a guy. We chatted for a few days online before exchanging phone numbers. After talking on the phone and getting to know each other, I found out that he worked with one of my best friends. So I decided to give her a call to inquire about him. When asked she said *"Girl, he is your type."* Sealing the deal for the date, she went on to say that he was a nice guy, highlighting the good qualities that she knew of him. At first, I was kind of paranoid and apprehensive about going out with someone that I met online. But, since I got the 'OK' from my friend I felt that I was safe.

Of course, I was very impressed with how well the date went. As soon as I got home, I deleted my Dating Profile Account. I thought for sure I met the man of my dreams. Things were moving fast. After dating for a few months, he met my children, and I met his. We became inseparable. Spending all of our free time together. We did family outings with our children. We were becoming a 'real family.'

The thing that attracted me and that I loved most about him was the way that he accepted my children who were from a previous relationship. He would always tell me that he felt that he was put in my life to take care of me. He also had this smile that would light up any dark room which also matched his infectious, outgoing personality. Everyone loved being around him. Not only that, but he was also a good provider and made me feel secure. The way that he would constantly compliment my looks and personality were also a plus.

Though enjoying the moment, things were really moving fast. About four months into the relationship we were having a general conversation when he looked over and said to me "Let's get married." Not too shocked by the question because of how good things were going, I said "OK." Happy, yet still playing in the back of mind were the times during the course of planning the wedding when I noticed that he would get angry and raise his voice at me. There were even times when he would talk to my children in a tone that I didn't like. But, I 'swept it under the rug' as him being stressed out because of the wedding plans and all of the changes that were taking place in our lives. A few months before the wedding we decided to start looking for a home that would accommodate our blended family. His children lived out of state, but they would visit us every other weekend and during certain holidays. He was very adamant making sure that we got the house that I liked. He wanted to make sure that I was happy and satisfied. Finally, we decided on a nice four bedroom home. We moved into the house three months before our wedding. I was indeed happy. I had my home, my family, and I was getting married for the first time in my life.

Soon after moving into our new home my fiancé began to talk to me as if I were one of the kids. He would yell at the children for no reason. He became very hostile and angry—all the time. His once loving tone of voice turned harsh and brash. What did I get myself into? He upsettingly became so mean that I was really starting to dislike him. Disturbed yet enabling, I justified and attributed his behavior to the stress of wedding planning.

As we got closer to the wedding date, the emotional and verbal outbursts began to get worse. He would walk around the house and not speak to me for days at a time. In the morning, as we would get dressed for work, he wouldn't speak to me or even say 'good morning.' Then, when I would say good morning to him, he would just look at me and roll his eyes. He began acting withdrawn, eerie and shared no regard for speaking to me in a very cold manner.

About two weeks before the wedding I began to have second thoughts, so I threatened to leave. He apologized for his behavior, convincing me to stay. As we got closer to the wedding date, my fiancé's attitude towards me got worse. He would look at me with disgust and roll his eyes at me. He would say things like..."You ain't all that." "I could do a lot better than you." But, because I had been engaged several times in the past I was too embarrassed to cancel this wedding. I sent the invitations out; my family booked plane tickets, and everyone was expecting a wedding.

The day of the wedding I maintained my composure, put on a fake smile and pretended to be happy. We looked each other in the eyes and said our vows like two people who were madly in love. We didn't even sleep together that night.

Over the course of the next three years my husband beat me emotionally, he beat me mentally, he beat me verbally, and he even beat me spiritually. He had been physical a few times by choking or restraining me. Although the physical abuse was not as often as the other forms of abuse, I feel that the emotional and verbal abuse had a bigger impact on me. It caused me to have a broken soul. Having a broken arm heals much faster than having a broken soul.

There are some things that I blocked out of my mind, and I do not remember. And some things are too painful to relive at this moment. I remember on several occasions being choked until I almost passed out. Thinking to myself, I'm about to die. But the most horrific incident was the day that I left. We were driving up the interstate, and I told him that I was leaving him for good. He got so angry that he forced the car to the side of the road where he began to hit, punch, and choke me. I think I passed out because the next thing I remember was being in the middle of the highway with cars swerving around me trying to prevent hitting me. Thankfully, someone saw what happened and called the police. I thought for sure I was going to die on that day. My life flashed before my eyes. I made it out, but not everyone does.

Trusting God and living according to Romans 8:28 has helped me to take my first steps on my path to survivorship. Everything that we go through in life has a reason and a purpose. Being able to turn my wounds into wisdom has given me strength and courage to live and to love again.

Since leaving my abuser, my life is full of freedom and peace. I am now living in my purpose of helping other women who are traveling the path that I survived! I am a full-time speaker, coach, and author, focusing on empowering women to live a life of passion, purpose, potential, and peace.

Are you sleeping with the enemy? If so, I encourage you to wake up before it's too late.

SURVIVOR TALK
Finding closure after abuse

Healing after an abusive relationship can be difficult. All breakups may have their aftermath of sadness and loss, but for someone transitioning from victim to survivor, the fallout may include continued harassment or attacks from the abuser. The resulting ongoing mental trauma and emotional stress can make a survivor question, "Was leaving really worth it?" Yes! Leaving is worth it.

Abuse is rooted in power and control, and an abusive partner holds that power by minimizing their victim's self-esteem and breaking their spirit. If you're leaving an abusive relationship, rebuilding your life can be a hard process, but with time and space, finding closure and peace is possible. A violence-free life is waiting, and you are so very worth it.

- If at all possible, cut off contact with your ex
- Surround yourself with support
- Take care of yourself
- Consider counseling

Meet The Authors

Tamara Charles

Tamara Charles is Founder & Chief Executive Officer of Sisters In Charge, a nonprofit organization for battered women with children based out of Georgia, that gives women a healthy start, the opportunity to learn and protection from harm. Ms. Charles takes her vision and makes it reality through sound strategy development. The mission of Sisters In Charge is to provide a safe shelter, and a variety of educational, recreational and social services to address the essential and changing needs of the families in Georgia and surrounding communities. Tamara Charles is a survivor of domestic violence and is currently living with multiple sclerosis. Her personal experiences allow her to understand the physical and psychological barriers that prevent many women from leaving their abusers. Ms. Charles also understands the potential fatal nature of domestic abuse, which makes seeking assistance imperative. By providing, a home where battered women and their children may seek temporary shelter, Ms. Charles hopes to help these women understand they are not alone. Her shelter will be designed to provide a safe space where victims may share their stories and meet other survivors to support them in their journey. Additionally, she hopes to provide these women with resources to help them gain control over their lives.

Venus Miller

My name is Venus Miller and I am a Family and Psychiatric Nurse Practitioner. My experience in nursing includes over 25 years of health care of patients over the life span. In 1990, I graduated from Barry University with a Bachelor of Science in Nursing. In 2003, I graduated from the University of Miami with a Master of Science in Nursing with a concentration in Family Nurse Practitioner. Currently I am Dual board certified family and Psychiatric Nurse Practitioner with a recent admission to the Doctorial program at FIU to begin Fall 2017. "STOP THE VIOLENCE NOW-IF YOU SEE SOMETHING SAY SOMETHING" is a campaign that is purposed to bring awareness to this national epidemic. My purpose is to empower the nation to make better choices and bring total physical & mental wellness. I know, from first hand, the trauma and long term effects of domestic violence and abuse as my mother died from the hands of my father when I was just 5 years old. The effects of that day opened my brothers and me to more abuse and trauma that would later affect all of our lives differently. Today, I stand delivered, set free, and with a voice to empower others after many personal failures, relationship losses, emotional and sexual abuse, divorce, and financial ruins, and I'm able to empower others to have a voice to live.

Yamma Brown Alexander

Dr. Yamma Brown was born in Augusta, Ga. The youngest daughter of Deidre Jenkins and James Brown, the Godfather of Soul. She attended high school at Archbishop Keough High School in Baltimore, Maryland and undergraduate training from University of Maryland at College Park, Maryland. She moved to Atlanta, Georgia in 1993 to attend Mercer University School of Pharmacy where she received her Doctorate degree at the age of 24. Dr. Brown has worked in the field of pharmacy for 12 years holding such positions as: Clinical Pharmacy Manager for Healix in Houston, TX, Assistant Director of Pharmacy/Clinical Director at Twelve Oaks Hospital in Houston, TX, as well as Director of Pharmacy at El Campo Memorial in Texas. She resided in Sugarland, Texas for approximately 5 years post graduate then relocated her family back to Atlanta, Ga. She has an extensive knowledge of several areas in the pharmacy arena, working in the hospital, retail, and long term care settings. She specialized in Infectious Disease, Neurology, Rheumatology, and Oncology. Dr. Brown states that even with accomplishing so much in pharmacy at a young age, family is most important to her. She has been very involved in her father's estate planning since his death on December 25, 2006. Her ultimate goal is to build his legacy so that the world is able to capture and feel the magnitude of his influence to civil rights as well as the music industry.

Detra Williams

Detra Denise Williams is a mother, grandmother and wife who currently works in Child Protective Service as a Forensic Social Worker at her Local Government Agency. Detra Williams is also an ordained minister, which earned her the title of an Evangelist. She is affectionately known as Evangelist Detra Denise Williams. Detra acquired her Bachelor's Degree in Social Work at age 47 after 5 years in college. After completion of her Bachelor's degree, she further pursued a Higher Degree, and in 2017 she obtained a Master's Degree in Human Services from Capella University. During that time, she was inducted as a member of Tau Upsilon Alpha-Beta Chi Honor Society. Detra's life has been about tolerance and endurance as she had to bear through the wounds of domestic violence. She believes this experience should be likened to an iron passing through furnaces, heat and pressure to forge a sharper sword. Detra's experience with domestic violence has made a stronger and more determined in life. On October 3rd 2016, Detra welcomed her first grandson and in him she finds joy and pride. 20 years ago she never believed she would be a wife, mother, grandmother and the most of all an ordained minister. For those who have a similar story to hers, she hopes her story will be a source of courage and strength to face and conquer the challenges and be a proud survivor of Domestic Violence.

Lakesia Muhammad

Lakesia Muhammad currently serves as the Lead Teller for a community bank in Central Florida but her passion lies in her love for the arts. As a highly requested singer and actress, Lakesia enjoys performing for social, religious, and community events in which her talents can be used to uplift and inspire her audience. Lakesia is no stranger when it comes to performing. She has had the opportunity to perform in many stage plays throughout the country, including New York and the Central Florida areas. Most recently she had the opportunity to co-star alongside Actor Carl Payne in the hit stage play, "My Prodigal Child" and has appeared on many media outlets including the local newspaper in Central Florida for her outstanding performances. Lakesia has a love for people and enjoys serving her community. As a Certified Breastfeeding peer counselor, she has the opportunity to provide a valuable service to her community, addressing the barriers to breastfeeding by offering breastfeeding education, support, and role modeling. As a domestic violence survivor and advocate, she believes that we are so much stronger than we ever give ourselves credit for. She is married to Latif Muhammad and has a blended family of seven children.

Roderick Cunningham

Roderick Cunningham is the Founder and Executive Director of the Beverly Cunningham Outreach Program, Inc. (BCOP). The Beverly Cunningham Outreach Program was founded in 2010 after Roderick's mother Beverly Cunningham Brown was shot point black in the head by her husband October 27, 2009. Domestic Violence has had a strong hold on Roderick's family dating back to his grandmother being shot at by her husband. Roderick has turned his pain into positive action by helping other victims, survivors and our youth to once again embrace a normalcy of life through the Beverly Cunningham Outreach Program and its partners. The mission of the Beverly Cunningham Outreach Program is to provide individual and group counseling, advocacy and rehabilitation services to survivors of domestic violence. The foundation also seeks to be an outlet for community youth who are at risk of becoming victims of violence, substance abuse or who are impacted by health issues. The program has helped over 4,100 children, women, and families through its domestic violence programs, economic empowerment programs, and community outreach programs from 2010-2013. Roderick has received numerous community service awards, resolutions and proclamations from the DeKalb County Board of Commissioner and state representatives.

Kimberly Claborn

My name is Kimberly Claborn. I am 27 years old. I am one of the 12 co-authors in, Wounds To Wisdom...The Survivor Series, Volume 2: In this book, I share how I have overcome being a childhood domestic violence victim, to helping my mom escape her 24 year abusive marriage to my father. I share the struggles along the way within our legal system, such as with Child Protective Services, and how law enforcement handles domestic violence cases, as well as how this has now become my passion and mission in life, to raise awareness on domestic violence. This endeavor has taken me all the way to The White House, local news, and a partnership with The National Domestic Violence Hotline as a guest blogger and various video content for their official YouTube channel. Dive into this amazing book and learn how I went from victim to overcomer and advocate!

April Kelley

"Favor is deceitful and beauty is in vain, but a woman that feareth the Lord shall be praised" These are the words that Ms. April Kelley lives by, words that have infused every aspect of Ms. Kelley's life. Ms. Kelley is a proud honor graduate of Benedict College (Cum Laude) and Argosy University, Atlanta Campus (Magna Cum Laude). Ms. Kelley was very active in college as well as in the performing arts sector in the community. Ms. Kelley's involvement with the arts organizations at Benedict College made her a well-known face on campus. She won the hearts of her colleagues and was elected and crowned Ms. Benedict College 2001-2002. During her reign, she was featured in Ebony and Black College Today magazines, and was recognized by the County/City Council as well as the Mayor of Anderson, SC for all of her hard work and dedication to her community. Currently, Ms. Kelley works with victims of sex trafficking and exploitation. Her professional experiences include teaching Pre-K, working as a Special Instructor/Early Interventionist with the Anderson County Disabilities and Special Needs Board, and Off Broadway Regional Productions. She is the voice and empowerment speaker for DIVAS In Defense and the Beverly Cunningham Foundation. Ms. Kelley was recently inducted as a trustee member into Rose Of Sharon ATL for Domestic Violence Survivors and the Queen Ambassadors USA, I am a Queen Foundation.

Duntenia Fitts

Poised with style and grace, Duntenia "Ms. Fitts" Fitts has a soft but commanding presence that you sense immediately when she walks into a room. Born in Los Angeles, California and raised in Rochester, New York, Ms. Fitts spent most of her early days at Faith Temple Apostolic church. She graduated high school from the School the Arts where she was classically trained in voice, piano and dance and was a part of a campaign that allowed her to act and also become a peer educator around the city of Rochester in hopes to prevent teen pregnancy and to educate on the dangers of becoming sexually active too early. Though Duntenia always desired to help others, she was once on the side of desperately needing help while being in an abusive relationship. She has experienced heartache and turmoil as a victim of domestic violence and because of it; Duntenia understands how her pain morphed into her purpose. "Through all of these trials and tribulations, she was introduced to her purpose. Duntenia spends a lot of her time volunteering at various events and shelters in the community and she also speaks throughout the community in order to inspire and uplift. Ms. Fitts is a walking success and desires to share with the world not only how to survive hard times, but to thrive after them. Ms. Fitts is a star not just because of her talents but because she shines bright enough to light someone else's mind and life.

Lakeisha Christian

LaKeisha Christian is a domestic abuse survivor and the founder of FREE (Fearless, Releasing, Executing, Expecting), an organization built to empower victims of domestic abuse to break the chains that bind their souls, minds and personal lives through activating truth found in the Word of God. She is a motivational speaker in the fight against domestic violence, sharing her personal experiences to encourage and educate others. She is also an aspiring author and entrepreneur. LaKeisha is a newlywed and spends her days in the lovely state of Virginia with her loving husband and children.

Pamela Morgan

Pamela Morgan is a wife, mother and an information technology professional who found her purpose after finding strength to leave an eleven-year abusive relationship. Pamela owes her survival to God who has protected her throughout the years and to this day calls on her to serve others through her life experiences. She believes her ordeal has a purpose and hopes her story of survivorship will help anyone who may be struggling in an abusive relationship to find the strength to leave. Everyone deserves to be happy and free. Born and raised in the Philippines until the age of 15, Pamela now resides in the Metro Atlanta area with her husband and their four blended children. She is a proud mother to two Airmen, a son and a daughter, in the US Air Force.

Kanorris Davis

Kanorris Davis is an American football safety and linebacker who is currently a free agent. He played college football for Troy University. Davis has played for the New England Patriots of the National Football League, with whom he signed as an undrafted free agent in 2013, and the Toronto Argonauts of the Canadian Football League. He attended Perry High School in Georgia and was a three-time first team selection for each all-district, all-area, and all-region teams. Kanorris currently coaches high school football in Troy, AL and enjoys writing poetry.

Tamiko Lowry Pugh

Tamiko Lowry-Pugh often referred to as "The Empowering Diva" is a voice for Women's Empowerment. As the CEO of EmpowerME! Life Coaching & Consulting - a personal development & lifestyle enhancement firm for women and the founder of The Still Standing Foundation – a nonprofit organization that that focuses on domestic violence awareness, advocacy, and prevention, she has constructed a powerful movement dedicated to the empowerment and personal development of women across the world. Tamiko is a member of The National Coalition of 100 Black Women, Inc., MECCA Chapter where she serves as the Public Policy Chair and an active member of Women In The Spotlight GoinGlobal. Over the years she has received many awards and recognitions including The 2013 Atlanta Rising Star Award for her work with the Still Standing Foundation. Most recently Tamiko received the Atlanta Black History Makers Award as well as the Unsung Heroine Award for her dedication to the fight to end domestic violence, just to name a few. As an International Bestselling Author, Inspirational Speaker, Empowerment Specialist, and Domestic Violence Educator, Tamiko believes that empowerment comes from within and can be achieved by honoring yourself, your values, and expressing your talents and gifts.

If there is no breaking then there is no healing, and if there is
no healing there is no learning.
~Wounds to Wisdom

Made in the USA
Columbia, SC
27 March 2018